Guide To Nantucket

Guide To
Nantucket

Third Edition

by
Polly Burroughs

The
Globe
Pequot
Press

Old Chester Road
Chester, Connecticut 06412

Cover design by Barbara Marks
Cover Photograph by Cary Hazlegrove
Book design by Kathy Michalove

Library of Congress Cataloging in Publication Data

Burroughs, Polly.
  Guide to Nantucket.

  Rev. ed. of: Nantucket, a guide with tours. 1st ed. 1974.
  Includes index.
  1. Nantucket (Mass.) — Description and travel — Tours.
I. Burroughs, Polly. Nantucket, a guide with tours.
II. Title.
F72.N2B95 1984   917.44'970443   84-47900
ISBN 0-87106-934-2 (pbk.)

Manufactured in the United States of America
Third Edition

*To Dave and to Ann whose Nantucket ancestry
began with Thomas Macy*

ABOUT THE AUTHOR

Polly Burroughs is a professional writer with a long-time understanding of island life. A year-round resident of Martha's Vineyard, she frequently visits nearby Nantucket which she knows as intimately as her own island.

Her eight previous books include Globe Pequot's *Guide to Martha's Vineyard, Zeb: A Celebrated Schooner Life, Exploring Martha's Vineyard,* and *Thomas Hart Benton; A Portrait.*

When she's not writing, Mrs. Burroughs enjoys such island activities as tennis, swimming, boating, and gardening.

CONTENTS

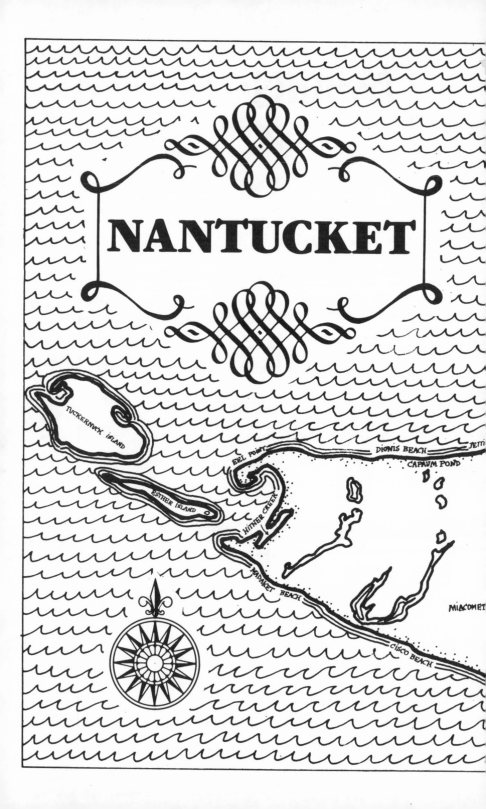

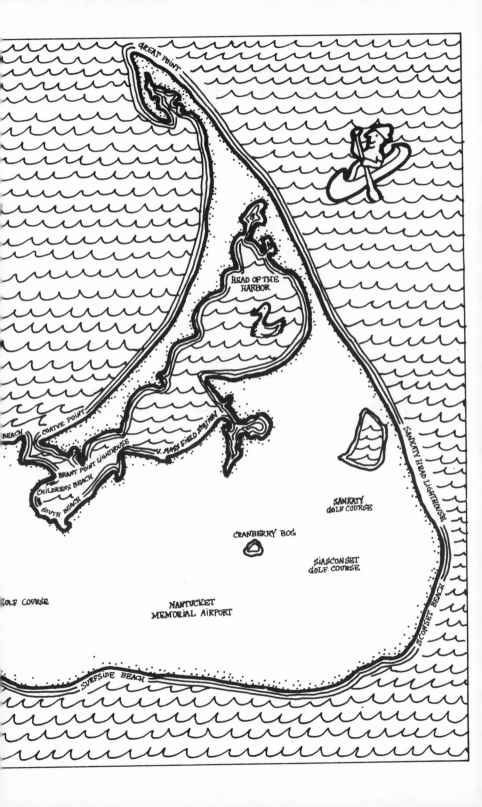

ACKNOWLEDGMENTS

The author is indebted to many organizations, as well as other individuals, who have been extremely helpful to me in putting together this Island guide. The Nantucket Historical Association, the Chamber of Commerce, the Director of the University of Massachusetts Field Station, the Nantucket Conservation Foundation, The Camera Shop, Sherburne Associates, individual craftsmen, and Island historians have all contributed to making it possible for me to tell Nantucket's story. And most important of all, my thanks to my patient editor, Cary Hull.

All selections of lodgings and restaurants have been made by the author. **No one can pay or is paid to be in this book.**

DO'S AND DON'TS

DON'T bring your car to the Island unless it's absolutely necessary.

DON'T plan to bring a camper to the Island. There are no public campsites or trailer parks on Nantucket. Sleeping in an automobile anywhere on the Island or sleeping on the beaches is illegal.

DON'T go barefoot in town. You will not be welcome in shops or public buildings, and the Board of Health has banned bare feet in all food establishments.

DON'T wear beach attire in the center of town. Swimwear is not considered the proper attire when shopping.

DON'T drive a moped or motor scooter in the Old Historic District between the hours of 8 p.m. to 8 a.m.

DON'T litter the streets, beaches, or roadways with trash of any kind.

DON'T drive on the town-owned portions of Cliffside, Dionis and Jetties Beaches.

DON'T plan to live on any sort of boat in Nantucket Harbor or Madaket Harbor or any of their creeks or estuaries without first obtaining a permit from the Board of Health.

DON'T pick any wildflowers. Many plants will die if their flowers are picked.

DON'T disturb any small clams, scallops, or other shellfish.

DON'T bicycle on the sidewalks.

DO watch out on the one-way streets in town. Most of them were laid out in the eighteenth century and they are narrow, sometimes bumpy, with high curbstones.

DO obtain a permit from the Fire Department before you have a cookout on the beach or in your backyard.

DO keep your dog on a leash at all times when in public.

DO obtain a permit from the Nantucket Conservation Foundation before taking your four-wheel-drive vehicle out to the Coatue Wildlife Refuge, Coskata-Coatue Wildlife Refuge, or the National Wildlife Refuge at Great Point.

DO keep your voice down in the town during the evenings. No shouting.

An Island for All Seasons

1

Twenty miles at sea from the south shore of Cape Cod, Massachusetts, lies the Island of Nantucket, which in Indian tongue means "land far out at sea" or "that far away isle." Approximately fourteen miles long and three and a half miles wide at its broadest point, this "little grey lady" as it was called by the whalers in the nineteenth century, is one of the most enchanting, architecturally unique spots in America. Its shape, like that of a huge whale flipping its tail, plus its simple beauty symbolize the Island's heritage — whaling and Quakerism.

This grey-green jewel with low rolling moors and miles of sandy beaches is surrounded by the sapphire blues of Nantucket Sound and the Atlantic Ocean whose continually shifting sands have shaped and reshaped its contours. And for over three centuries, the sea, the wind, and the tide have molded her human history as well. It was the ocean that spawned Nantucket's great era of wealth from whaling and made possible the exquisite architecture of the historic houses. It is the ocean today that brings the Island its wealth from tourism.

With one port of entry the town of Nantucket is a perfectly preserved New England seaport containing hundreds of authentic eighteenth and nineteenth century homes, unlike any other place in America. The town has cobblestone streets wending their way down to the waterfront, brick sidewalks lined with handsome wineglass elms and gaslights. The historic houses are close together in the English tradition with their fences giving a continuity of line. Their old fashioned gardens are edged with English boxwood and roses covering picket fences.

Strolling along these narrow streets and twisting lanes on a quiet fall evening, with the whiff of woodsmoke tinging the salt air, is just as if one had stepped back a century in time, or stumbled onto a movie set for a nineteenth-century film. Restaurants in old taverns or cellars visible from the street have fires lighted, and the flickering light from the hearth plays on the beautiful antique furnishings. The twentieth century only seems to intrude sporadically here, such as in the selections in the attractive shops and the most modern yachts along the waterfront.

Beyond Nantucket town there are little pockets of settlements scattered among the low rolling moors that stretch seaward in every direction. Grey weathered houses, in keeping with the Island's traditions, are scattered through the landscape. There are vast tracts of open land, due to the diligence of the Nantucket Conservation Foundation, where a multitude of varieties of birds and some wildlife may be seen. The plant life and blankets of wildflowers are a nature lover's delight.

There are four seasons in which to enjoy Nantucket. Each season has certain characteristics that have evolved through the Island's long and fascinating history.

Beginning in early June, tourist travel to Nantucket accelerates rapidly from the 6,000 to 7,000 winter residents to about 45,000 summer residents, not counting the hotel guests and hundreds who come in on the daily cruises from Cape Cod. With several hundred places to stay the town is very crowded in July, and especially so in August, and reservations are a must for anyone contemplating a visit. The swimming in Nantucket Sound or Atlantic ocean waters is superb, and there are also fishing, golfing, tennis, sailing, and other sports to enjoy.

Because of the surrounding sea which is slow to warm up and slow to cool off, autumn lingers, reluctant to yield to winter until after Christmas. September and October are beautiful; those halcyon fall days when a yellow haze hangs over the moors in the mornings, middays are filled with a false warmth, and the nights are pierced with cold. The fields are ablaze with goldenrod and purple aster, flocks of migrating wildfowl and songbirds touch down to rest, Arctic birds settle in for the winter months, and boats are hauled in for winter storage. The moors are sheathed in fall colors accentuated by the vivid red of the high bush blueberry which is everywhere.

For the visitor the beaches are no longer crowded, the water is still warm and hearty swimmers find the ocean delightful until mid-October. While some places do shorten their hours, most of the restaurants are open through mid-October at least. The blue and bass fishing is in its prime, and the days are still pleasant for boating, sports, and nature walks. In late fall one can see the scallopers getting their old wooden workboats ready for another season of dredging the bottom of Nantucket

In the late fall the scallopers are busy dredging for scallops (left).
In the springtime, painters keep busy preparing for the summer tourist season (below).
A stroll by the moonlit water around Nantucket is an enjoyable way to spend an evening (right).

M.C. WALLO

FRANK FALACCI

M.C. WALLO

Harbor and out along Tuckernuck Island for scallops.

By December, the time of Nantucket's Christmas Walk, the Island has returned to itself, regaining its small town character with small town rhythms. This is what the native Islanders prefer, and what their ancestors were accustomed to for generations, living close to the soil and the sea. Nantucketers put a lot of time and thought into preparing for the Yuletide, and the center of town looks like an exact replica of a nineteenth-century Christmas card. The annual Shoppers Stroll, on the second weekend of the month, is a highlight of the season. Fifty-five Christmas trees line the cobblestone square, mulled cider, cookies and sherry are offered in the shops brimming with Christmas gifts, while horse-drawn carriages take visitors around town to admire the handsome traditional holly and evergreen decorations on these historic houses. Candles are lighted in all the windows on the second floor in the Main Street Square, Santa and caroling enhance the festivities until the whole town sparkles with the holiday spirit. Down on the waterfront fishermen hoist Christmas trees to the masthead to celebrate the holidays.

Midwinter is very quiet on Nantucket and bone-chilling winds sweep across the Island. While the winters aren't as cold as those on the mainland, because of the Gulf Stream, and are usually comparable to those in Philadelphia or Washington, the dampness is penetrating, and the days grey and bleak. Many homes have been closed for the rest of the winter, many shops and restaurants are closed, and about half the artists and craftsmen go South to return with their work in the spring. For those who do stay, it's a busy time painting, knitting, weaving, sewing, sculpting, and designing furniture. For the visitor there are some lectures, films, and sporting events at the local high school which are of particular interest to Island residents. It's a quiet time, but for someone who likes to walk an empty beach, curl up with a good book by the fire in one of the lovely old inns, or spend the evening with a local inn-keeper learning about the Island, it can be very enjoyable.

And out on the moors, with snow and ice silhouetting the Island's contours with its marshmallow coating over the marshes, the Island looks very beautiful and completely different from midsummer. Occasionally the harbor ices up, sometimes thick enough to prevent the ferries from running for several days. Then Nantucket's silent solitude is abruptly broken by news reports from the mainland that the Island is isolated from "America," and people may have to be evacuated. The old-timers are always amused by these exaggerated reports and go right on coping, just as they have for three centuries, while airplanes bring in any essentials. Economically, scalloping is the important source of winter income and the fishermen are busy on the good days out in the harbor harvesting the delicacy to be shipped to the mainland. Don't be surprised to see a hurriedly scratched sign on a shop door which says, "By chance or by appointment. Gone Fishin'," or simply, "Gone Fishin."

That sapphire blue sea which makes the fall so pleasant and turns a raw, pewter grey in winter, keeps spring at bay, so it comes late to the Island. The days are cool and crisp, and the white gulls soaring against the bright blue cloudless sky that is exceptionally sharp and clear at this time of year signal the start of another season. As the days begin to get longer and warmer, the Island begins to waken to the rhythms of nature and the pace quickens. The birds return to their nesting sites, and shad bush and the popcorn flowers of the beachplum sprinkle their delicate white blossoms across the moors. Nantucket finally celebrates the rites of spring with the Daffodil Walk in late April when the roadsides, gardens, shops and parks all burst into bloom. Some, but not all, of the Island accommodations and restaurants open for the Daffodil Walk,

The snow on the Three Bricks enhances the beauty of these historic houses.

and there are golf, tennis, horseback riding, and walking the beaches for the visitor to enjoy. Swimming is unlikely, however, for it's not until late May or early June that a hearty swimmer might be brave enough to jump into the chilly ocean.

The most familiar ritual on these beautiful spring days is the smell of fresh paint and the sound of hammers as many young men and women are out painting, scraping boats, fixing fences, or repairing houses as they ready the town for another season, which begins officially on Memorial Day.

A Nantucket vacation is enjoyable for all ages, but the elderly might prefer to wait until spring or mid-autumn when the large crowds are gone. It would also be difficult for the elderly to get around during

Nantucket's beaches are very popular in the summer and fall.

the Shoppers Stroll in December when snow might be a problem. The center of town could be difficult for the handicapped to manage. Cobblestoned Main Street with its high curbstones and brick paving isn't as easy as smooth surfaces for canes and wheelchairs.

One of the most frequently asked questions by a first-time visitor to Nantucket is who lives on the Island in winter and what do they do. Descendants of the original families are now engaged in real estate, insurance, banking, gift shops, fishing, building, and shipyard work. There is a large group of retirees who have summered here for years and now are year-round residents. Many spend a few months in the midwinter in the South. Other year-

M.C. WALLO

round residents include the children of people who have summered here for years who prefer Nantucket to urban life.

So whether you prefer midsummer with all the resort activities, the semi-quiet warm fall days, the midwinter solitude and cold, or the crisp spring days with that cool, prevailing Southwest wind coming off the water, you'll find Nantucket is an island for all seasons. This guide is designed to help you discover some of the Island's great charm whatever your means of transportation, the season of the year, or the length of your stay.

A Brief History

2

"And thus have these naked Nantucketers, these sea-hermits, issuing from their anthill in the sea, overrun and conquered the world like so many Alexanders..."

MOBY DICK Herman Melville

While there are many legends about the origin of Nantucket, the favorite involves the giant Moshup, an Indian tutelary divinity who lived on Cape Cod. He is said to have tossed his sand-filled moccasins out to sea one sleepless night to create the islands of Nantucket and Martha's Vineyard. Another story tells of Moshup knocking the ashes out of his pipe, which settled down on the sea to make the Island.

Nantucket's natural formation came about during the last Ice Age. The first mention in recorded history of this terminal moraine of sand and gravel was made in 1602 by Bartholomew Gosnold, the English explorer who had discovered Martha's Vineyard. He vaguely described the course of his vessel in relation to Nantucket. But it was George Waymouth, another Englishman, who gave the nautical position of Nantucket in 1604, and mentioned the "whitish sandy cliffe" of Sankaty Head, although he didn't go ashore. Had he done so, he would have seen the low moorland, long stretches of sandy beach, huge, protected harbor, ponds, kettle holes, coves, and lagoons populated by Indians who belonged to the Narragansett tribe of the Algonquin family.

In 1641, Thomas Mayhew of Watertown, Massachusetts, purchased for forty pounds Martha's Vineyard, Nantucket, and the Elizabeth Islands from two English noblemen who held conflicting grants to these islands. With his son, and others, Mayhew planned to establish a manorial system of land tenure similar to those in England, and to convert the Indians to Christianity. The group settled in Edgartown on Martha's Vineyard, and its members, as well as Vineyard Indians who had been converted to Christianity, visited Nantucket from time to time, becoming acquainted with the Indians who lived there.

It was in 1659 that Tristram Coffin, a planter living in Salisbury, Massachusetts, north of Boston, surveyed the Island and opened negotiations to purchase it from Mayhew. Coffin and a group of friends strongly resented the rigid code of the Puritans in the Boston area and sought the freedom of their own community. Because of the untimely death of his son and consuming work on Martha's Vineyard, Mayhew agreed to sell all of Nantucket except for a small portion at Quaise. A deed was drawn up on July 2, 1659 by which Mayhew sold to the nine Salisbury purchasers his patent "for the sum of thirty pounds in good Marchantable Pay in ye Massachusetts under which government they now Inhabit . . . and two Beaver Hatts, one for myself and one for my wife . . ."

These nine original buyers included Tristam Coffin and his son, Peter, Thomas Macy, and Messrs. Folger, Swain, Hussey, Barnard, Greenleaf, and Pike. According to William Macy's history of Nantucket, published in 1923, each person, including Mayhew, was given a share. To encourage more people to join the settlement, each original proprietor was granted another share to allow him to choose a partner. Then they issued fourteen half-shares to craftsmen, in return for their skills for the proposed settlement. Thus, the group became known as the twenty-seven original shareholders under whom all the land of the Island, except Mayhew's property at Quaise, was held in common for many years. In subsequent years the full-share men and half-share men would engage in many bitter battles to wrest political control from one another.

Thomas Macy was the first of the group to leave the mainland for Nantucket. He was a Baptist, and had found religious prejudice in the New World nearly as bad as it was in the Old World. He had gotten along well in the community, despite the Puritans' intolerance, and being kindhearted, had allowed some Quakers to take refuge in his house one stormy day. This was reported to the Puritan authorities who had been so distrustful of the rapidly growing Society of Friends that they had passed a law making it a criminal offense for anyone to entertain Quakers. Macy was fined, and two of the men he had taken in were hanged for professing their religion. Macy needed little urging to leave, and in the fall of 1659 made the voyage from north of Boston in an open boat with his wife, five children, a friend, Edward Starbuck, and twelve-year-old Isaac Coleman.

Their landfall, near Madaket on the western end of the Island, allowed for a quick exodus toward the

Vineyard should they encounter any trouble with the Indians. However, the Algonquin natives, who were divided into the territories of Sachems Potconet, Autoscot, Wauwinet, and Wanackmamack treated them kindly, which was not only their disposition, but Mayhew had already planted the seeds for peaceful coexistence.

Because of the sandy, gravelly soil and relentless winds, the Island had few trees, and one can only imagine the settlers' first lonely, bleak winter in a

Captain Charles Myrick, *oil on canvas, by Eastman Johnson, 1879.*

Captain Myrick, who was in the coastwise trade, was a favorite model of Eastman Johnson. Johnson was one of several well-known artists who used to visit Nantucket in the late nineteenth century. The Peter Foulger Museum has two other Johnson paintings.

crudely built cabin with small children to feed and keep warm.

The following spring others began to arrive from Salisbury until, by the end of the year, there were sixty settlers in all. They settled in the area near Capaum Pond, a little harbor in those days that is now landlocked. They called the area Sherburne, a name which lasted until June, 1795, when it was changed to the town of Nantucket.

The hospitable Indians taught these new arrivals what they knew of fishing, killing wildfowl, and

17

Abram Quarry, *oil on canvas, by Hermione Dassel*

The last male Indian on Nantucket, Abram Quarry put on a coat and cravat for the painting, although he discarded his shoes. Abram lived alone on the Island and made baskets for sale.

farming, and introduced them to the Island's wild cranberries. The settlers, in turn, repurchased their tracts of land from the natives as specified by Mayhew and worked to educate these Indians who ultimately paid dearly for this generosity. The Indians soon realized they had forfeited necessary use of their lands for grazing and other purposes, and spent years, in vain, trying to reclaim them. Both the disease of the white man and his "firewater" took their toll in the end. The last male Nantucket Indian, Abram Quary, died in 1854.

Obed Macy, in his 1843 *History of Nantucket* laments the tragedy: "In the simple charity of nature they rescued our Fathers. When fugitives from Christian persecution they opened to them their stores, bestowed on them their lands, treated them with unfailing kindness, acknowledged their superiority, tasted their poison and died. Their only misfortune was their connection with the Christians and their only crime, their imitation of their manners."

The first group of settlers included many skilled half-share men — a carpenter, joiner, miller, shoemaker, tailor, farmer, seamen, and others — to make the growing community as self-sufficient as possible. They imported only those things they couldn't make or grow themselves. Sheep and cattle were introduced and grazed freely on the common lands. Farming was of subsistence level with very poor soil, and they were glad to learn the art of shore whaling from the Indians.

It was inevitable they would turn more and more to the sea for their livelihood. In 1712, when Captain Christopher Hussey was blown out to sea, he came upon a school of spermaceti whales and managed to harpoon one. Until this time only Right whales (so-called because they were considered the right whale to kill), were being hunted close to the shore. Hussey's chance encounter set the course which was to eventually make Nantucket the whaling capital of the world. These Islanders perfected deep-sea whaling, excelling in the art of harpooning the huge mammal, sometimes one hundred feet long, from a small whaleboat. Once harpooned, the whale usually sped off angrily on a perilous "Nantucket sleigh ride" through the ocean until it was worn down. Other times it knocked the whaleboat to kindling wood in a matter of seconds, or rammed the whaleship itself again and again until the vessel was sunk. It was an extremely dangerous business, which one whaleman said extracted "a drop of blood for every drop of oil," and they endured mutiny, cannibalism, stench, suffering, and sacrifice in their global voyages which could last years. But a "greasy" trip meant huge profits to be shared — to many, well worth the risks and hardships.

As the hunt for sperm oil grew, the Islanders began to relocate into the town above the harborfront, which was rapidly expanding with the building of warehouses, candle factories, rope walks, and other businesses related to whaling. For a century and a half whale hunting controlled the Island's economy while the Quaker religion dictated its way of life, even the architecture. The original settlers had sought total freedom from Puritan ways, and for fifty years after their arrival there was no formal religion of any kind, although Quaker missionaries from England often visited the Island. But in 1708, Mary Coffin Starbuck, a very strong influential woman, the type Nantucket had to manage the home and town affairs while the men were away at sea for months at a time, became a Quaker and organized the Monthly Meeting of Friends in her home. She attracted many followers. The Quaker philosophy of pacifism, personal liberty, temperance, and hard work, and the belief that a spiritual intermediary was unnecessary, appealed to these independent Islanders. As whaling and the Quaker faith dominated the community, even their language became a curious mixture of Quaker and nautical expressions.

Captain Fred Parker, c. 1880

After a life at sea, accustomed to small quarters and months of solitude, some seamen who had no families continued a reclusive existence when they retired. Captain Fred Parker was known as the hermit of Quidnet, where he spent his last days.

The Quakers were opposed to slavery, so by the 1770's there were only a few slaves on the Island. One was named Boston, who was owned by William Swain. On Boston's return from a whaling voyage aboard the *Friendship,* the Swains claimed his share of the profits should go to them. William Rotch, one of the most prominent and successful Islanders at the time, owned the *Friendship* and was not going to tolerate this injustice. He went to court, defending Boston, and won his case, striking the first blow for emancipation of blacks in the state, a century before the Civil War. Soon after that there were no more slaves on the Island.

There were Portuguese-blacks living on the Island who had been recruited as crewmen on whaleships when they had stopped in the Cape Verde islands off the coast of Africa. By 1820 there were 275 blacks listed in the Nantucket census of 7,300 residents. Most of them lived on upper Pleasant Street which was known as "New Guinea."

The blacks were excellent crewmen, for the most part, and there were many in the crew aboard the whaleship *Brothers* when it was trapped by a storm off the coast of New Zealand. With the stern to the rocky shore and an impossible headwind, Captain Benjamin Worth met with his officers to consider whether they should continue to try to get the vessel out of there, or run it aground. Word spread quickly through the vessel and the black sailors to a man went to Captain Worth and begged him to try once more. They knew from other sailors that the cannibals in this particular part of New Zealand preferred dark meat. The captain agreed to try one more time, and fortunately the weather broke and the whaleship escaped.

Cannibalism was such a part of life in the Pacific during those early years that William Endicott in his 1820's journal described the Fiji Islanders' method of cooking bodies, similar to a clambake. A hole was dug in the sand, hot coals were spread out, wet leaves and layers of flesh were put in with old mats spread over them to confine the steam, and "in twenty minutes the flesh was cooked."

Yet not all South Sea Islanders were hostile. Hawaiian women adored the Nantucket sailors and would swim naked out to the whaleships when they sailed into port. A whaling captain was not adverse to reminding a restless and difficult crew that in no time they would be in the Hawaiian Islands.

A Quaker whaling wife was so overwhelmed by the lush beauty and flowers of Hawaii, compared to Nantucket's winter, that she wrote home: "I thought I had died and gone to heaven."

During the last part of the eighteenth century, Nantucketers were carrying on a very lucrative trade with England, shipping oil, ambergris, and candles to London. (In fact, it was the crime in the streets of London that helped the Nantucket economy as much as anything, for the Londoners put in street oil lamps to try to improve the situation.) Things were going very well indeed, until 1773, when three Nantucket ships, *Beaver, Dartmouth* and *Eleanor,* having taken cargoes of oil and candles to London, returned to Boston loaded with tea, which was thrown overboard during the famous Boston Tea Party.

As the Revolutionary War gained momentum, Nantucketers tried to remain neutral, because the Quakers were pacifists, and also economically dependent on England with many social and blood ties. At the same time, they were fiercely independent, proud to be Americans, and geographically in an impossible position where they were vulnerable on both sides. Finally, a large number of Islanders rallied to their country's cause and served on American ships, but they paid a heavy price. When they returned home after the war, they were disowned by the Quaker church. Having been distrusted by both sides in the war, the Islanders suffered heavy losses from both the Americans and the British.

After the war, recovery was slow and many impoverished citizens really suffered, while others left the Island. But the whaling fleet was gradually rebuilt, and when the whaleship *Beaver* rounded the Horn in 1791 and opened the Pacific to whaling, Nantucket's industry prospered once again. Nantucket whalemen lived on the Pacific for months on end, more familiar with the Fiji Islands or Hawaii than Nantucket where they now spent only a brief time with their families. They had to rely on their strong and capable Quaker women, dressed in coal scuttle bonnets and shawls, to manage the children, and run their homes and many of the town's affairs.

This prosperity was short-lived, however, with the outbreak of the War of 1812. Nantucket's fleet numbered 116 vessels, and with the memory of the Revolution still fresh in their minds, Nantucketers were horrified to be in the middle of another war. They were defenseless, the Quakers were pacifists, and determined to take no active part in the war. The Islanders tried to keep on good terms with both sides, with the natural result that they were trusted by neither. Ships were seized by both the British and French navies and the Island was blockaded. Losses were severe, leaving only twenty-three vessels in the fleet. For about three years Nantucket was in a severely depressed state, as it had been after the Revolution, but gradually the fleet was built up once again. With the discovery of the lucrative Japanese whaling grounds after the war, Nantucket forged into its golden era.

The harbor was jammed with whaleships; some fitting out for another long voyage, others unloading their barrels of oil and rolling them into one of the large warehouses. Not only were casks of oil exported to light the lamps of half the world's capitals at that time, but also whalebone for ladies corsets, candles made at the twenty-four candle factories in town, and the precious ambergris, used for perfume and fine soap, were shipped to England, France, and other countries. The harborfront was crowded with industries relating to whaling: sailmakers; shipyards; blacksmith shops fashioning razor-sharp harpoons and lances for the dangerous work ahead; rope walks; coopers making barrels for oil; and bakeries making hardtack for the long voyages of these "blubber hunters."

It was during this period of enormous prosperity when every whaleman worked on a "lay" system, sharing in profits from these successful voyages, that Nantucket's stately mansions on Upper Main Street were built by the merchants who owned the whaleships. (The whaling captains, who endured all the hardships, lived in houses such as those on Orange Street where a hundred were supposed to have lived at one time.) The shipowners' houses were furnished with precious silks, Indian rugs, oriental porcelains, Chinese furniture, and other elegant furnishings from what became known as the China Trade. Concerts, lectures, and other cultural activities flourished during this period of great affluence, while the Quaker traditions of simplicity slowly diminished.

These whaling voyages that lasted up to five years required larger vessels which drew so much water they were unable to get over the shoals marking the

The William Hadwen Houses, c. 1880
COURTESY OF DUKES COUNTY HISTORICAL SOCIETY, MARTHA'S VINEYARD

It was during the prosperous whaling era in the 1830's that many Nantucket mansions were built. The two Hadwen Houses, the most imposing Greek Revival houses in the town, were called the "two Greeks" across the street from the "Three Bricks."

entrance to Nantucket Harbor. Although a "camel," a drydock arrangement, was built to lift them over the bar, it proved unworkable. The ships were soon obliged to fit out at Edgartown on Martha's Vineyard, or New Bedford which eventually became the whaling capital of America.

Nantucket was still at the peak of her whaling days when a fire broke out on Main Street in 1838, destroying some of the buildings. It was followed eight years later by the fire of 1846 that completely gutted the center of the town, burning more than 300 buildings. All the businesses along the waterfront that were connected with the whaling industry went up in flames. As the town struggled to rebuild after this devastation, word of the California Gold Rush spread through the maritime community. As a result, many Nantucket seamen jumped ship in California eager to join the march to the gold fields. Nantucket whaling masters had difficulty shipping competent crews. With the Island's economy in such dire straits, it's surprising that Nantucketers put so much thought into rebuilding after the fire. The buildings on the Main Street square were well built, and they widened the cobblestone street to prevent another similiar catastrophe.

But the discovery of petroleum in 1859, followed by the Civil War during which the whaling fleet was virtually destroyed, dealt the final, fatal blow to Nantucket's industry. In a few short years, her two-century economy was dead.

While the rest of New England entered into the Industrial Revolution following the Civil War, Nantucket lay dormant. Many of the houses were shuttered and abandoned, deteriorating from neglect. Docks were crumbling and grass grew between the cobblestones on the side streets. Some houses were moved off-Island on coast-wise schooners, those broad-beamed, gaff-rigged vessels used to move freight under canvas all along the eastern seaboard.

The remaining inhabitants, with stalwart determination and reserve, earned a living from commercial fishing, shellfishing, harvesting cranberries, and some sheep husbandry. Attempts at industrializing Nantucket failed, sparing the Island unsightly mills and adjacent slums, as well as much Victorian architecture. These were harsh times, but gradually another business began to emerge which would eventually become the Island's economic salvation.

Beginning in the mid-nineteenth century, saltwater bathing became the rage for vacationers who previously had enjoyed the supposed therapeutic value of mountain watering places with mineral springs. Hotels began to spring up on the Island, in the town of Nantucket as well as one in the outlying village of Siasconset, and the first newspaper advertisement for a cottage to rent was in 1865. Tourism was just a trickle at first, but it soon flourished and grew until it became the Island's primary business.

That long impoverished period, that pause in its time cycle while its history lay dormant in the dark and empty houses became, in the long run, Nantucket's most valuable asset. By losing its economy, and by being relatively isolated as an island, Nantucket preserved its character. By the time it became a well-known resort, the newcomers who bought and restored the houses found this perfectly preserved heritage from the eighteenth and nineteenth centuries to be priceless and invaluable.

How to
Get There

3

Because Nantucket is an island, getting there takes a little more planning than just getting in a car, but there is always a certain excitement about an island vacation. The most commonly used transportation to the Island are the ferries from the Cape Cod towns of Hyannis or Woods Hole. The town of Hyannis, located midway along the south shore of Cape Cod, is about a 45 minute drive from the entrance to the Cape. This drive can take considerably longer during the summer, especially on weekends. Hyannis is about 80 miles from Boston, 187 miles from Hartford, Connecticut, 270 miles from

New York, and 500 miles from Washington, D.C. Woods Hole, which is at the beginning or shoulder of the Cape, is about a 45-minute drive directly south from the bridge over Cape Cod Canal.

Car

Driving from Boston to Hyannis or Woods Hole takes about two hours, but you should allow more time in the heavy summer traffic. From downtown Boston take the Southeast Expressway (Route 3) to Sagamore Bridge over the Cape Cod Canal. Take the Mid-Cape highway (Route 6) to Route 132 which leads on down to Hyannis. If you're going to Woods Hole, from the Sagamore Circle take Route 28 over the Bourne Bridge to Falmouth. Follow signs to Woods Hole.

Driving from New York City may take six hours. Take Interstate 95 to Providence, Rhode Island; Route 195 to Wareham, Massachusetts; Route 28 to the Bourne Bridge over the Cape Cod Canal. Follow Route 28 to Falmouth and proceed on to Woods Hole. If you are going to Hyannis, take Route 6 alongside the canal to the Sagamore Bridge. Continue onto the Mid-Cape Highway (still Route 6) and then to Route 132 to Hyannis.

Train and Bus

Amtrak train service goes to Providence or Boston; from there you must arrange for other transportation to Cape Cod. Bus service is provided to Hyannis and Woods Hole from the New York City Port Authority terminal (212-564-8484), the Boston Greyhound terminal (617-423-5810), and from Providence on Bonanza Bus Lines (401-751-8800).

Ferry

Once you've arrived in Hyannis, you have two choices of ships (the Steamship Authority and the Hy-Line company) to take you over to Nantucket. From Woods Hole, you have only one choice, the

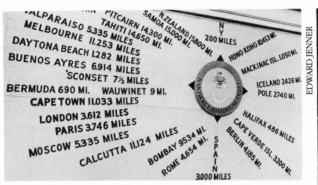

Nantucket can be reached from all points of the compass.

Steamship Authority. Choose the ship you'll take according to your need for your car on the Island; only the Steamship Authority allows cars on its ferries.

Newcomers to the Island frequently ask, "Should I bring my car?" The Chamber of Commerce, Selectmen, and other town officials urge you not to bring your automobile if your visit is short and you are staying in the town of Nantucket itself. The Main Street area becomes extremely congested in July and August and with the availability of taxis and buses, or rental bikes, mopeds, and cars, you will find it much more convenient not to have an automobile to worry about. However, if your stay is for a week or more, or you are planning to be in the outlying areas on the Island such as Siasconset, Wauwinet, or Madaket, you will want your car.

The Woods Hole, Martha's Vineyard and Nantucket Steamship Authority operates daily ferries from Hyannis and Woods Hole to Nantucket, carrying passengers as well as cars and trucks. It is a two and one-half-hour trip from Hyannis and a three-hour trip from Woods Hole. During the summer, there are four regularly scheduled ferry departures from the dock in Hyannis and one from Woods Hole, per day. The Woods Hole ferry leaves at 7:15 a.m. and makes a stop at Martha's Vineyard. Between mid-September and June, the ferry schedule is quite different, so always call ahead to determine current schedules (617-540-2022).

Reservations for automobiles on and off the Island must be made weeks or months in advance by phoning the Steamship Authority's office, but passengers do not need reservations. Always allow ample time to get to the ferry. (You must be at the dock at least 30 minutes prior to sailing time if you have a car reservation.) If you decide to leave your car on the mainland, give yourself plenty of time to find a parking place. It costs $4.50 per day to park in the Authority's parking lot, or in the Hy-Line's parking lot nearby.

Transportation costs on the Authority's ferries from Woods Hole or Hyannis are as follows, but are subject to rate increase:

Round trip automobile fare	$95.00
(from Oct. 15-May 14)	65.00
Adult passenger one-way fare	8.00
Child (5-15) one-way fare	4.00
Off-season adult one-way fare	7.50
Off-season child one-way fare	3.75
Bicycle one-way fare	4.00

The Hy-Line company runs four boats a day for passengers and bicycles only from its Ocean Street dock in Hyannis during the summer and fall, and three a day in the spring. No reservations are necessary. To determine its schedule, call the Hyannis office (617-775-7185) or Nantucket office (617-228-3949). The fares for passengers and bicycles are the same as the Steamship Authority's.

During the midsummer, the Authority ferry and the Hy-Line boats may be loaded to capacity. If you use the Hyannis wharves and find one ferry is filled, you can easily walk over to the other wharf to check on the other company's ship.

Private Boat

If you own a boat and plan to cruise on it to Nantucket, call ahead to make a reservation for a slip or a mooring. These are difficult to obtain during the summer, so it's advisable to call as far in advance as possible.

All the slips at the Nantucket Boat Basin are owned by Sherburne Associates. Phone jacks, showers, electricity, and laundromat are available to boat owners at these slips. For further details, call the Dockmaster (617-228-1500). Nantucket Sail (617-228-4897) and Nantucket Shipyard (617-228-0263) have moorings to rent by the day. Launch service in the harbor is provided by Nantucket Sail, and by Nantucket Yacht Club (for members and guests only). If you need to reach the Nantucket marine operator, call 617-228-4692. (For VHF Marine calls, dial operator and ask for the Nantucket marine operator.)

Plane

Another way to get to Nantucket is in a plane. There are several airlines with direct flights to the Island from Northeast cities, or you can drive part of the way to the Island and fly the rest of the way.

It is becoming increasingly popular for people coming from New York, New Jersey, and points south to fly from New Bedford, Massachusetts, directly to the Island. This avoids all the Cape Cod traffic, saving one and a half hours of driving time. It is a relatively inexpensive — $30 one way — and quick — one-half hour — plane ride. Parking is free at the New Bedford airport, and there are many flights a day during the summer.

Another alternative is to fly from Hyannis. There are flights almost every half hour during the summer. From the late fall until spring all the airlines sharply reduce the number of flights.

PBA (Provincetown-Boston Airlines) is the largest air carrier serving the Island. It has direct flights to Nantucket from Boston's Logan Airport, New York's LaGuardia Airport, New Bedford, and Hyannis. For information call 1-800-343-0330 (in the Northeast), or call 617-771-1444.

TOM LANDERS

M.C. WALLO

*Many Nantucket visitors come to the Island in their own
boats (left).
The Steamship Authority's ferry, the Naushon, brings
visitors to Nantucket from Cape Cod (bottom left).
As you cruise into Nantucket Harbor, be sure to notice
Coatue, the long, scalloped barrier beach on your left
(below).*

EDWARD JENNER

Gull Air has flights to Nantucket from Hyannis, New Bedford, Massachusetts, Boston, and Martha's Vineyard. For reservations call 617-771-1247 (in Massachusetts call 800-352-7191).

Wills Air has flights from Hyannis and Boston. For reservations call 617-771-1470 (in Massachusetts call 800-352-7559).

Atlantic Air has a direct flight from Bridgeport, Connecticut, to Nantucket. Phone 800-243-9830 (in Connecticut, call 800-972-9830).

The following are the average airline prices for a one-way ticket, and are always subject to change.

Boston-Nantucket	$45
Newark-Nantucket	79
New York-Nantucket	75
New Bedford-Nantucket	30
Hyannis-Nantucket	20
Martha's Vineyard-Nantucket	20

For those flying in their own planes, Nantucket Memorial Airport is tower-controlled between 0600 and 2100. Runway 6-24 (6300 feet long) has an instrument landing system. Fuel is available 24 hours daily (80-100-Jet "A"). Overnight parking and tie-downs are available as well as aircraft repair and servicing facilities.

* * *

Whether you take a plane or boat to the Island, you'll find the trip a memorable experience. From the air, the sculptured blues and greens of the sea and the meandering sandy shoals dotted with white sails are a beautiful sight. The Island looks open and undeveloped, and the long stretches of white sandy beaches and clear water are very inviting.

The ferry ride is equally delightful, perhaps even more so for the newcomer, for it is a unique way of becoming acquainted with the islands that surround Nantucket. The ferry ride is an extremely pleasant cruise down Nantucket Sound in good weather, and food and liquor are available.

As the ferry cruises down Nantucket Sound, the large island on the starboard side of the vessel (your right) is Martha's Vineyard. This island is twice the size of Nantucket and has become an equally popular summer resort. The last easily identifiable point is the lighthouse at Cape Pogue on Chappaquiddick Island which is part of Martha's Vineyard. As the island passes from view the ferry continues out into Nantucket Sound towards the Gulf Stream which is responsible for Nantucket's mild climate. In fact, it was Benjamin Franklin, who with the help of a whaling captain cousin, first charted the Gulf Stream in 1769. Franklin's grandparents, Peter and Mary Morrill Folger, were members of Nantucket's founding families, and his mother, Abiah, was born and raised on the Island.

As the ferry approaches Nantucket, the sea's colorful collage of blues and greens is deceptive. The waters here are extremely shoal, and with the strong currents that swirl around the Island, this has been one of the worst ship graveyards on the Eastern seaboard. A New Bedford newspaper once estimated that between 1843 and 1903 over 2,100 vessels had been wrecked on Nantucket shoals alone!

The first sight of land, a low purplish streak on the horizon on your right, is the deserted, privately-owned Muskeget Island. Coming into view to the left of Muskeget is the sparsely settled Tuckernuck Island, also privately owned, then tiny Esther Island created by the 1954 hurricane. As the ferry moves on, Great Point, the narrow, northern tip of Nantucket, becomes visible off the ferry's port bow, while the sandy cliffs off the starboard bow are the Dionis Beach area. The 166-year-old Great Point Lighthouse stood here until it disappeared in a storm in March, 1984.

A blinker marks the entrance to the jetties which protect the channel into Nantucket Harbor. The land on your left is Coatue, a long, narrow, scalloped barrier beach known for its acres of beautiful beach roses, prickly pear cactus, and cedar trees sculpted close to the ground by the prevailing southwest winds. This area is best seen from the ferry, and can only be reached by boat or jeep from Wauwinet. The ferry slips between the jetties, rounds the famous Brant Point light, and cruises on into the wharf.

How to Get Around

4

It is not essential to have your own car to enjoy the Island. At the wharves as well as at the airport, taxis, buses, bicycles, mopeds, and cars are available for transportation.

Taxis

There are quite a few taxi companies on Nantucket, some operate only in season, others are year round. The yellow pages of your phone book lists them all; the following are familiar year-round companies:

Gail Nickerson, 228-0179
Barrett's Taxi Service, 228-0174

Bicycling is the most popular way to get around Nantucket.

Peterson's Taxi, 228-9227
John's Taxi, 228-4084
J.H. Wood & Son Taxi, 228-0133

A taxi ride from the airport, which is 2½ miles from town, costs $5.00 for one passenger, and an additional $1.00 for each additional passenger. It costs $7.00 for a taxi ride from town to Cisco, Madaket, and Quaise; $9.00 to Siasconset, Quidnet, and Pocomo; and $10.00 to Sankaty Head and Wauwinet. All rates are subject to change.

Buses

Barrett's Tours (228-0174) provides regular bus service from its office at 20 Federal Street to Jetties Beach, Surfside, and Siasconset, from June 15th to Labor Day. Their buses run about every half hour until early evening, but from Thursday through Saturday they run until late evening. Their prices are $1.75 from town to Surfside, $4.00 from town to Siasconset, and 50¢ from town to Jetties Beach.

Barrett's also offers six different sightseeing tours of the Island daily, spring through fall. For over sixty years, members of the Barrett family, descendants of Nantucket's whaling captains, have owned and operated this bus company which also has taxis, car rentals in season, and private limousine service.

Island Tours, on Straight Wharf (228-0334), provides sightseeing tours of the Island from April through November. Carol and Gail, mother and daughter, also give tours in their Volkswagen buses to small groups or individuals. Call them at 228-0179 at least one day in advance to arrange for a two-hour tour. You can find them on Lower Main Street, parked in front of the 5&10. Their tours are available year round.

Bicycle, Moped and Automobile Rental

If you come to the Island during the summer, especially in August when it is most crowded, it is advisable to rent your bicycle, moped or car in advance. Be aware, however, that the main part of town during the summer becomes extremely congested, and a car here becomes a nuisance.

Nantucket lends itself to bicycling, as it is relatively flat, and most areas are within easy reach. There are bicycle paths from town out to Surfside

COURTESY OF MASS. COMMERCE & DEVELOPMENT, DIVISION OF TOURISM

The streets are narrow on Nantucket Island, so you'll want to leave your car at home and rent a bicycle or go by taxi.

and Siasconset, and bicyclists must use them instead of the roads. Riders of bikes and mopeds are cautioned to pay close attention to Nantucket's rules and regulations and violators now receive tickets. Mopeds may not be used on bike paths, one-way street signs should be observed, and no bike riding is allowed on sidewalks. If you are riding after dark, the law requires front and rear reflectors, and it is advisable to also have a light. Mopeds and motorcycles are prohibited in the Old Historic District between 8 p.m. and 8 a.m. Both cobblestoned Main and Liberty streets are impossible to bike, so it's best to use the nearby parallel streets. Riding on sandtracks and dirt roads is extremely hazardous; there have been many accidents.

In 1983 it cost $35.00 per day to rent a car, $6.00 to rent a bicycle, and $20 to rent a moped ($16 per half day).

Distances from town to the outlying areas are:

Life Saving Museum	2½ miles
Quaise	4 miles
Polpis	6 miles
Wauwinet	5½ miles
Quidnet	7 miles
Siasconset	7½ miles
Surfside	2½ miles
Cisco	4½ miles
Madaket	5½ miles
Dionis Beach	2½ miles
Jetties Beach	1 mile
Airport	2½ miles

Various vehicles are available for rent from the following companies:

Young's Bicycle Shop, Steamboat Wharf and Airport, 228-1151. Something of an institution on Nantucket, the third generation of Youngs are now working in the business. They are most helpful, witty and tourist-wise. Open all year, they have bikes, mopeds and Ford cars for rent.

43

The "Argonaut" at Nantucket Boatyard

Avis, Straight Wharf and the Airport, 228-1211 (Seasonal)

Island Motor U-Drive, Washington Street, 228-4150 (Seasonal)

Colonial Car Rental, Airport, 228-0135 (Year round)

Nantucket Jeep Rental, Macy Lane opposite Airport, 228-1618 (Seasonal)

Preston's Rent-A-Car, Somerset Road, 228-0047 (Year round)

Island Rentals, North Beach Street, 228-4316 (Seasonal)

Thrift Cars, Airport, 228-1227 (Year round)

Nantucket Bike Shop, Steamboat Wharf, 228-1999 (Seasonal)

Where to Stay

5

If you are planning a visit to Nantucket, the earlier you make your reservations the better; January is never too soon. If you wait until spring, chances are you may not be able to find any housekeeping units, particularly for August, and the best hotel suites and cottages may have been reserved.

With tourism the source of Nantucket's economy today, the Island has many possible accommodations for visitors — hotels, inns, apartments, private guest houses, and small rental cottages. There also are houses available for rent. There are not, however, any public or private campgrounds, and camping of any sort is prohibited on the Island.

Visitors who want to pay by the night for an accommodation should stay at a hotel, inn, or private guest house. These are available in a wide price range, often based on whether meals are included in the price. For instance, some Nantucket accommodations are on the European Plan (EP), rooms without meals, while others provide room and full breakfast. Modified American Plan (MAP), room with breakfast and dinner, is available at some of the inns. Guest houses on Nantucket correspond to what is called Bed-and-Breakfast in other areas, usually providing continental breakfast.

The inns and private guest houses do not lend themselves to small, active children. Most of them were formerly private homes and are furnished with antiques. The hotels or other places that are on the beaches, or that provide lawn areas and swimming pools for children to romp in, are much more relaxing for everyone.

Visitors staying at least one week will probably choose an apartment or cottage. Apartments, usually consisting of bedroom, living room, and kitchenette, are available in some of the guest houses as well as the hotels. Rental cottages are usually very small and simple, and may be part of a hotel complex, or a cottage community.

Generally, the rates for private guest houses range from $20 to $40 per person per night in season (June 15 to October 15). Rooms and suites in the inns and hotels range in price from $55 to $350 per couple per day. Cottage and apartment rental rates vary depending on location, type, and size. Typical rates are from $400 per week for two persons and from $600 per week for two bedrooms. Off-season rates for all accommodations are usually ten percent or sometimes twenty percent less.

Some private homes are available for rent through Nantucket real estate offices. Prices for monthly or seasonal rentals range from a few thousand dollars to $15,000, or more.

There are three accommodation services on the Island that can be most helpful in helping visitors locate a place to stay.

Nantucket Accommodations is a reservations service that lists many, but not all, of the guest houses and hotels on the Island. They will describe the facilities to you over the telephone and make a booking for you. They are at 6 Ash Lane, and their phone number is (617) 228-9559.

Nantucket Vacation Rentals, at the same address, is a service listing some cottages, apartments, and houses to rent. Call them at (617) 228-3131 for more information.

Nantucket Information Bureau is a town-operated information bureau that puts out a detailed brochure on everything from places to stay to car rentals. They will not make reservations for you, but they do keep track of hotel vacancies. They are at 25 Federal Street, and their phone number is (617) 228-0925 or 228-0926.

The following accommodations are just a small sampling of the many delightful places to stay on Nantucket.

Hotels and Inns

The White Elephant
Easton Street
(617) 228-2500
Seasonal. EP.

The White Elephant is a lovely, sprawling hotel complex running along the west side of Nantucket Harbor between the Steamboat Wharf and Brant Point. There is a main building with regular hotel rooms and dining facilities. There are also several clusters of small cottages, a short distance from the main building, some of which have kitchens. Another building in the complex is The Breakers, which is the most expensive and elegant of all the White Elephant's accommodations. It consists of sitting/bedrooms, some with views of the harbor, and suites with private patios. Guests in The Breakers are greeted with wine and fresh flowers in their rooms. Complimentary continental breakfast and afternoon wine and cheese are included in the room fee at The Breakers. A concierge is on duty 24 hours a day to assist guests with everything from renting a sailboat to making a dinner reservation.

The White Elephant has its own docking facilities, small putting green, and swimming pool. It is a very easy place to manage children, and it is a very short walk to the center of town.

Jared Coffin House
29 Broad Street
(617) 228-2400
Open year round. EP.

In 1845, the Jared Coffin House was built so sturdily of English brick with a roof of Welsh slate that it was saved from the devastating fire in 1846. It was the first three-story house on Nantucket and was built by Jared Coffin as a futile attempt to keep his wife happy on the Island. It became an inn in 1847 and ever since has been an Island landmark. Over the years several other buildings have been added to the hotel complex to increase the number of guest rooms. Furnished with beautiful antiques, such as the large Cinnibar lamps in the lobby, the inn has a famous embroidery room and a formal dining room. Its taproom with heavy, old, dark beams and pine paneling is a typical nineteenth-century tavern.

Harbor House
South Beach Street
(617) 228-1500
Open April through December. EP.

Located very close to Main Street, the Harbor House is an attractive, courtyard-type hotel complex consisting of the main hotel and several cottages and houses. The hotel also owns one fully equipped house for rent by the week. There are lovely gardens, a charming patio where breakfast and lunch

49

Jared Coffin House

Built in 1845 by one of the Island's most successful ship-owners, the Jared Coffin House has been a very popular inn since 1847.

are served, and a heated swimming pool. Entertainment is provided nightly in the lounge. Harbor House has a special spring package for the Daffodil Walk, and another special package for any autumn weekend. Both the Halloween Ball and the Daffodil Ball are held here in the hotel.

India House
37 India Street
(617) 228-9043
Open April through December. EP.

This historic house, formerly the mansion of ropemaker Charles Hussey, was built in 1803. It is located close to the center of town, but is in a quiet spot with a delightful, peaceful garden out back. All the guest rooms in this charming inn have private baths, four-poster beds, and some have working fireplaces. The restaurant here is award-winning and is famous for its delicious Sunday brunches.

The Woodbox
29 Fair Street
(617) 228-0587
Open May through October. MAP.

Built in 1709, The Woodbox is Nantucket's oldest inn. It has the hand-hewn beams, huge fireplaces with ovens, and low ceilings that are so typical of eighteenth-century houses. The rooms are beautifully furnished with period antiques. The restaurant serves breakfast and dinner.

Ships Inn
Fair Street
(617) 228-0040
Open year round. Continental breakfast included.

Built in 1812 by Captain Obed Starbuck, this charming whaling captain's house is located in a quiet area, which is still very close to the center of town. It is beautifully furnished with antiques. Many of the rooms are named for ships under Starbuck's command. The house was also the birthplace of Lucretia

Coffin Mott, the first woman abolitionist and advocate of women's suffrage. The inn has a delightful lounge and excellent restaurant serving dinner.

Beachside Motel
North Beach Street
(617) 228-2241
Open year round. EP.

This comfortable motel is a rarity on Nantucket, but typical of many in America. Its location is convenient to Jetties Beach, yet it's an easy walk to town and restaurants. There are 52 double rooms, each with modern furnishings, a refrigerator, color television, and cablevision. There also are three efficiency units with kitchen facilities available. The large courtyard makes this a relaxed place for families with young children.

Overlook
Three Step Lane
(617) 228-0695
Open May through October. EP.

This old-fashioned hotel, called the "Veranda House" in the 1880's, is just a few more than three steps from the center of town, and not far from Jetties Beach. Still, it is in a quiet, delightful spot and has been recommended by several magazines as a good place to stay. The rooms are large and airy, and almost every one has a porch and looks right out on Nantucket Harbor. The restaurant, the Indian Room, is well known for its traditional, hearty country breakfast featuring New England Fried Bread Dough.

Private Guest Houses

Nantucket's private guest houses, known as Bed and Breakfast accommodations elsewhere in the country, have become increasingly popular on the Island. All the ones listed below include continental breakfast in their room fee.

Harbor House

*Located at the end of a typical Nantucket street with
grey weathered buildings, brick sidewalks and gaslights,
the Harbor House is built in an attractive courtyard-
type complex.*

M.C. WALLO

House of Orange
25 Orange Street
(617) 228-9287
Open year round.

The House of Orange is located on the street where so many whalemen lived in the nineteenth century. It was built in 1810, and each room has charming antiques. Some of the rooms share a bath. There is a lovely, intimate, terraced garden.

House of Seven Gables
32 Cliff Road
(617) 228-4706
Open year round.

A ten-minute walk from Main Street, the House of Seven Gables is located a few blocks from the beach, and most rooms look out to the sea. This Victorian house is a rarity on Nantucket, and there are eleven rooms for guests, all decorated in period furniture. It was built originally as an annex for the Sea Cliff Inn, one of the Island's first hotels which no longer exists.

The Carriage House
4 Ray's Court
(617) 228-0326
Open year round.

One block off Main Street on a quiet country lane, and a stone's throw from the Pacific Bank, this delightful guest house has been recommended by several travel guides. A tastefully decorated white clapboard house, it was converted from an original carriage house. It has a nice game room and a flower-filled outdoor patio with tables and umbrellas.

The Four Chimneys
38 Orange Street
(617) 228-1912
Open April through December.

This handsome, historic house was built in 1835 and became an inn in 1856. Larger than many Nantucket guest houses, it has eleven guest rooms, nine with private bath, and most have a fireplace. It is furnished with canopied and four-poster beds, and rugs and porcelains from the China Trade. Set-ups and hors d'oeuvres are provided at cocktail time.

Phillips House
54 Fair Street
(617) 228-9217
Open year round.

Just a six-minute walk to Main Street, the Phillips House is in a quiet location. There are four guest rooms in this typical Quaker house, one with private bath. The owner, who is a basketmaker off season, extends favorable winter and early spring weekly rates to summer job seekers.

Rita Kip Ayer
78 Main Street
(617) 228-1185
Open June through September.

This is indeed a departure from the average Bed and Breakfast place. Rita Kip Ayer is a New York hostess who lives at the Ritz Towers in New York City. She was formerly the shopping editor for *Harper's Bazaar*. She has recently turned her Georgian home on cobblestoned Main Street into a guest house. Three guest rooms are available at $100 per night per person. The guest is treated to an exquisitely decorated home, and continental breakfast is served on silver trays, with beautiful china and flowers, in either the sunroom or out in the garden.

Fair Gardens
27 Fair Street
(617) 228-4258
Open May through October.

This is another of those charming Nantucket Quaker houses in the historic district that has become a delightful guest house. It is in a nice quiet location, but at the same time is very close to town. There are six guest rooms, most with private bath, and some with a fireplace. The grey stone wall, rose arbor, and lovely, old fashioned English country garden where breakfast is served, provide just the setting a visitor to Nantucket would hope to find.

Apartments and Cottages

The following apartment and cottage accommodations are in addition to the ones that are part of the hotels listed in the Hotels and Inns section.

The Gray Goose
24 Hussey Street
(617) 228-1530
Open mid-June through Columbus Day.

This exceptionally attractive eighteenth-century house, across from the Old North Church, is just far enough away from the center of things to be quiet, while still remaining within easy walking distance of everything. There are six suites, and English and American antiques and charming period piece fabrics are used throughout. For those who want to prepare some of their own meals, there is a kitchenette and dining area as well as a place in the flower-filled garden and patio to grill fish or meat. A

Nantucket Waterfront

one-week stay is the minimum, and no children under 13 are permitted.

Wharf Cottages
Swain's Wharf and Old South Wharf
(617) 228-4620
Seasonal.

For many yachtsmen, these cottages owned by Sherburne Associates on the harborfront wharves are a welcome respite ashore, while their boats are tied up at a slip outside the door. The cottages are very close together and very popular, so it's best to make reservations weeks or months in advance. They are large enough for two to eight people, and include kitchen and dining area. Many have private decks. Linens are provided.

75 Orange
75 Orange Street
(Reservations through Nantucket
Accommodations.)
Open April through December.

There are two spacious two-bedroom apartments and two single rooms in this conveniently located house just off Main Street. The rooms are bright and sunny, with considerably more modern furnishings than Zimri Cathcart, a "Master Mariner" had when he purchased it in the mid-nineteenth century. The apartments are available on a weekly basis, the rooms daily, and there are laundry facilities and maid service if you wish. Towels and linens are provided in the apartments.

Accommodations in the Outlying Areas

To stay in one of the various places in the outlying areas fringing the shoreline of Nantucket requires transportation — a car, moped, or bicycle. While Siasconset does have one small grocery store, most supplies must be bought in Nantucket town. There is also a grocery store at Hither Creek in Madaket.

The Wauwinet House
Wauwinet
(617) 228-0145 (in winter, call 617-744-7365)
Open May through October. EP and MAP.

This is a typical, large, turn-of-the-century hotel at the head of Nantucket Harbor, six miles from town. It overlooks the gentle harbor bay, and a very short walk through the dunes leads over the barrier beach to the ocean. It is a wonderful place for children and offers tennis, sailing, and a fine restaurant. There are no housekeeping units.

58

The Summer House
Siasconset
(617) 257-9976
Open May through October. EP.

The Summer House is located in an attractive setting on a bluff on the edge of the sea. It consists of a

Evening fishing

main hotel building and tiny grey shingled cottages. An oddity for Nantucket, but something some visitors will enjoy, is a swimming pool right on the beach below the bluff. Lunch or cocktails may be enjoyed on the sand here. Lunch and dinner are served six days a week, and there's also a fine Sunday brunch in the hotel's restaurant.

Bartlett's Beach Cottages
Hummock Pond Road, Cisco
(617) 228-9403
Open year round.

These tastefully furnished housekeeping cottages, a few minutes walk from both the ocean and Hummock Pond, are owned by the Bartlett family which has the well-known vegetable gardens. The minimum rental is for two weeks in the summer, pets are allowed, and pond boats are provided. They are located four miles from town.

59

M.C. WALLO

Wade Cottages
Siasconset
(617) 257-6308
Open May through mid-October.

Formerly a private estate, Wade Cottages consist of rooms with private or semi-private baths, apartments with one to four bedrooms, and cottages with three to five bedrooms. The grounds are spacious and attractive with a sea view and private beach. Tennis, golf, and restaurants are nearby.

Youth Hostel
Surfside
(617) 228-0433
Open April through October. EP.

This is, of course, a very popular spot for bikers and backpackers. It is located in the old Life Saving building on the beach. To stay here, membership is required, and the introductory pass is $2 per night. There are 72 beds, cooking facilities, and it is open from 5 p.m. to the curfew at 10:30 p.m. The maximum stay is for three nights.

Grieder Waterfront Cottages
Madaket
(617) 228-1399
Open May through October.

There are many houses for rent on this western end of the Island, but very few small cottages available by the week. Grieder is one of the few, with two nice cottages on Madaket Creek, each consisting of two bedrooms. For those who like a very informal, beachcombing and fishing type of holiday, this is a nice area of the Island.

Dionis Cottages
Dionis Beach
(617) 228-4524
Open year round.

Just two miles from town, these five larger cottages, one with four bedrooms, have central heat, fireplaces, complete kitchen facilities, and linens. They are right on the beach of the North Shore where the swimming is gentler than in the ocean.

The Taylor Cottages
Madaket
(617) 228-0519
Open May through October.

There are four attractive housekeeping cottages here, only yards away from the surf and good fish-

61

Ships Inn
The stark and spare influence of the Quakers is very apparent in this four-square building. The picket fence and sidelights by the front door are the only exterior departures from this austerity, while inside the inn exudes delicious food and warm hospitality.

ing areas. One cottage has three bedrooms, the rest have two. Cots are available. Rentals are for two weeks minimum. Sailboats are available for guests, and for those who want an informal holiday on the beach, these tastefully decorated places are ideal.

Cliffside Beach Club and Hotel
Jefferson Avenue
(617) 228-0618
Open May through October. EP.

Directly on Jetties Beach, less than one mile from town, there are both hotel rooms and housekeeping apartments at the Cliffside. Tennis, sailing, and lounging on the beach make this a very pleasant place to stay.

Wherever you decide to stay on the Island, there are a few basic facts you should know. In most cases, pets are not welcome in Island accommodations. Always check with the owner or manager of the hotel, or wherever you will be staying, if pets are permitted.

If you're planning a visit in the spring or fall, be sure to bring both summer and light woolen clothing. The weather can be very changeable during these seasons. The fall, however, is pretty certain to stay warm because of the surrounding ocean that is slow to cool off. A very light coat or sweater will be needed in the evening any time from May to October.

Where to Eat

6

The number of restaurants in Nantucket has increased rapidly the last few years until there are now about fifty, all varying in size, price, and specialties. The following is a small sampling of the many choices available in the various price ranges. All the more expensive restaurants prefer their customers to be appropriately dressed with the men in ties and jackets and the women in dresses or dressy slacks. Be sure to inquire about payment; some places won't take any credit cards or personal checks, others take only certain credit cards.

Very Expensive

Chanticleer
Siasconset
257-6231

Most people familiar with Nantucket consider this the Island's premier restaurant. A car, taxi, or the Island bus from Thursday through Saturday (although the last one leaves the village at 10:45 p.m.) is necessary to get to this charming rose-covered cottage. The classic French food includes pheasant, quail, and bass and other seafood. Lunch is served in the old-fashioned garden. There is a prix fixe for dinner, and a pianist is in the attractive bar every night. The Chanticleer is open for lunch and dinner from the end of May to mid-October, and reservations are required.

Company of the Cauldron
7 India Street
228-4016

This lovely restaurant specializes in Northern Italian cuisine. It is open for dinner only, with two seatings for which reservations are required. The harp accompaniment is very pleasant. The restaurant is open from May to mid-October, Tuesday through Sunday. No credit cards or checks are accepted.

India House
37 India Street
228-9043

One of the Island's best restaurants, India House is also a charming inn. Serving both dinner and breakfast, it is particularly known for its Sunday brunch, as well as its elegant breakfast which includes whiskey pears, Bourbon French toast, grilled boneless quail, and berries in champagne. India House is open seven days a week, April to December, and the *Boston Globe* gives it three stars!

De Marco
9 India Street
228-1836

Delicious Northern Italian cuisine is served here. The menu lists many pastas and entrees in Italian with a full description in English for each. It is open for dinner, six days a week, mid-May through mid-October. Reservations are suggested.

Straight Wharf Restaurant
Straight Wharf
228-4499

Only seafood entrees are served here, and each one is light and elegant. All the rich desserts are made on the premises. Meals are expensive, with a minimum entree charge per person. The restaurant serves dinner only, Tuesday through Sunday, and is open from mid-June through September. It has a nice bar that opens in the late afternoon.

Expensive

Jared Coffin House
29 Broad Street
228-2400

The dining room of this renowned inn is formal in atmosphere with handsome period furnishings. It serves traditional food. The pine-panelled taproom downstairs is a well-known gathering place for Nantucketers and serves fine chowder and hamburgers. The inn is open year round for breakfast, lunch and dinner, and there is music every evening in the bar. As one of the Island's best known hostelries, it is definitely a place you should see.

The Thistle
20 Broad Street
228-9228

Open from April through December, this attractive restaurant serves international cuisine, including rabbit, beef, lamb, duckling, and seafood dishes.

Dinner is served from 6:30 p.m. on, seven days a week, and reservations are requested. There are smoking and non-smoking dining rooms.

Obadiah's
2 India Street
228-4430

Located in an 1840's whaling captain's house with lovely antique furnishings, Obadiah's serves all the local fish including Tuckernuck mussels, codfish curry, and striped bass from that section of the south shore near Surfside which is known as Nobadeer. Both luncheon and dinner menus are extensive and the restaurant is open from April to mid-December.

The Boarding House
Corner of Federal and India streets
228-9622

The charming nineteenth-century atmosphere of The Boarding House makes this an attractive setting for lunch or dinner. The upstairs features à la carte dinners; the downstairs serves à la carte lunch and dinner. Dinner is also served on the attractive patio in the warm weather. The menu is always changing, and offers Island-fresh fish and vegetables. The restaurant is open from March through December, Monday through Saturday. Reservations are requested.

Harbor House
South Beach Street
228-1500

This restaurant is located in the Harbor House hotel complex, near its swimming pool and patio where children may wander while parents are having cocktails. The menu features good traditional food with local fish specialties. Complimentary champagne is served with Sunday brunch. The restaurant is open year round for breakfast, lunch, and dinner, and there is nightly entertainment with dancing in the lounge. Reservations are requested.

Club Car
1 Main Street
228-1101

You can't miss the old railroad train down by the wharf that has been converted into the Club Car restaurant. It has a wonderful atmosphere. The bar opens at noon and has a piano player every night. The restaurant opens for dinner at 6:00 p.m. and features an inviting selection of fish, beef, and lamb dishes. It is open year round.

M.C. WALLO

The Brotherhood
This restaurant, known for its character and good food, is one of the most popular places on Nantucket.

Nantucket Waterfront

Le Languedoc
24 Broad Street
228-2552

This is a small, charming restaurant in a cellar with a lovely garden terrace. The handsome blue tiles around the fireplace, blue-checked tablecloths, and well-situated serving bar make dining here a pleasure. In the summer, meals are served on the lovely garden terrace. Private dining rooms are available for parties of 8 to 12. Reservations for dinner are required. It is open year round, seven days a week, serving three meals a day.

69

The Woodbox
29 Fair Street
228-0587

A little out of the way, but well worth the walk, this 1709 inn radiates Nantucket's past. It is small, intimate, and famous for its popovers. The restaurant is open from mid-June to mid-October for breakfast and dinner, Tuesday through Sunday. Dinner is served in two seatings, by reservation only. The restaurant has a beer and wine license. No credit cards are accepted.

Moderate

The Brotherhood
23 Broad Street
(no listed phone)

Famous for its chowder and hamburgers, The Brotherhood has, according to several Island natives, the most atmosphere of any Nantucket restaurant and is therefore one of the most popular places on Nantucket. The name of the bar, "Brotherhood of Thieves," is taken from a pamphlet written by Stephen S. Foster on Nantucket in 1843, which was titled, "The Brotherhood of Thieves: or A True Picture of the American Church and Clergy." It is open year round, seven days a week for lunch and dinner. No credit cards are accepted.

The Nantucket Lobster Trap
23 Washington Street
228-4041

The Lobster Trap is known for its seafood, especially its lobster, which many Islanders feel are the best big lobsters on the Island. It is open spring through fall, and offers a Happy Hour bar, and dinner from 5:30 p.m. on. There is a nice outdoor patio here. The Lobster Trap also offers a unique service called "Meals on Keels" which is a clambake to go. They will deliver it to your home, boat, guest house, or motel, or you may ask to be transported with your clambake to the West End public beach. What a pleasant and unusual way to entertain!

Atlantic Cafe
15 South Water Street
228-0570

This is a great gathering place for young year-round residents. It has a great deal of atmosphere with its old tavern tables and heavy hand-hewn beams.

Prices are very reasonable and meals are simple, with the same menu for lunch and dinner.

Cap'n Tobey's Chowder House
Harbor Square
228-0836

What this restaurant lacks in atmosphere, it makes up for in its simply cooked fish and chowder and its reasonable prices. Open spring through early fall for lunch and dinner, the early-bird special served from 5:00 to 6:30 p.m. is a daily feature.

The Captain's Table
13 Fair Street
228-0040

The Captain's Table restaurant in the historic Ships Inn serves tempting entees with such dishes as fresh Nantucket fish of the day. The Dory Bar has all the character and charm one would hope to find in a nineteenth-century inn. The restaurant is open from mid-April to mid-November, six days a week (closed Tuesdays). Reservations are requested.

The Mad Hatter
72 Easton Street
228-9667

This is one of the very good year-round restaurants on Nantucket, and a favorite with many residents for lunch and dinner. The menu offers old favorites such as chowder and local fish, and there is a buffet on Sundays.

Arno's
Center of Main Street
228-4098

Arno's has very reasonable prices for all the familiar fish dishes including bluefish, scrod and sole, as well as cheese or tuna sandwiches. It serves breakfast, lunch, and dinner from May through October, as well as providing take-out foods.

The Upper Crust
9 West Creek Road
228-2519

If you go up Main Street and turn left on Orange Street and head out of town, you will come to West Creek Road and The Upper Crust restaurant and bakery. Here is a delightful restaurant well worth your trip which serves beef, duckling, fish, and other traditional entrees. It is open for breakfast, lunch, and dinner, year round. It also has a bakery which is open all day, Tuesday through Saturday.

Main Street

When you're hungry for a quick snack, the produce trucks on Main Street are a good place to look.

North Shore Restaurant
80 Centre Street
228-0397

Open seven days a week from April through December for breakfast and dinner, the North Shore restaurant serves very good and very reasonable food. Some past specialties were the Mount Vernon Farm vegetable pie and the broiled Nantucket scallops. The breads and pastries are freshly baked on the premises.

PAUL J. CONNELL.

Back with scallop catch
You'll find wonderful fresh fish and shellfish at Nantucket's restaurants.

Snacks and Take-Out Food

Claudette's Catering
On the Square in Siasconset
257-6622

Claudette's is open year round for catering parties, weddings, and dinners. It also is open seven days a week, during the summer to provide box lunches, canapes and party foods, and clambakes to go.

The Dory
10 India Street
228-9824

This is the ideal spot for an early riser who would like a 6:00 a.m. hearty and inexpensive breakfast. There are also omelets and quiches to take out for lunch, and it is open, as the advertisement says, "until the chicken croaks." The Dory does not have any old Nantucket atmosphere, just a counter and simple tables and very efficient service, as well as an outside terrace where, they claim, "the elite meet to eat."

Patisserie-Marty
Oak Street
228-0060

Delicious French pastries, croissants, and quiches are served in this charming little spot with its small, round tables. Beer and wine are available. It also has all sorts of sandwiches to take out, as well as some beverages. Birthday cakes are available on order, which is particularly nice for those living aboard boats. It is open year round, Monday through Saturday, from early morning to late afternoon.

The Blueberry Muffin
Centre Street
228-9740 or 228-3941

Freshly baked donuts, pastries, and muffins are ready early each morning here. It also serves lunches of soups, sandwiches, and hamburgers, as well as ice cream sodas and sundaes, to eat here or take out.

Something Natural
50 Cliff Road
228-0504

The huge, tasty sandwiches here will appeal particularly to men, as they are truly double-size. The store also has lots of natural foods, delicious salads, homemade breads and cakes to take to the beach, as well as soft drinks, coffee, and tea. It is located so conveniently for those on their way to Jetties Beach, and it is seasonal.

The Downy Flake
South Water Street
228-4533

Nantucketers are very partial to this restaurant which has its own bakery. It is renowned for its doughnuts and moderate priced traditional food. It is open for breakfast and lunch, as well as for take-out food, from April through December.

Telephone Numbers & Addresses

7

For your basic needs during your stay on the Island, here are some telephone numbers and addresses you will want to keep on hand.

General

For *emergency* only — fire, police, or ambulance, call 911
Congdon's Pharmacy, 47 Main Street, 228-0020
Nantucket Pharmacy, 45 Main Street, 228-0180
Nantucket Cottage Hospital, So. Prospect and Vesper Lane, 228-1200

Police Department, East Chestnut Street, 228-1212
Fire Department, Pleasant Street, 228-2323
M.S.P.C.A. (Animal Hospital), Crooked Lane, 228-1491
U.S. Post Office, Federal Street, 228-1067
U.S. Post Office, Siasconset, 257-4402

Churches

There are twelve churches on Nantucket, one of which is in Siasconset.

Baha'i, 43 Fair Street
Christian Science, 8 Gardner Street
Congregational, 62 Centre Street
First Baptist, Summer Street
Friends Meeting, 7 Fair Street
Jehovah's Witnesses, Milk Street Extension
Lighthouse Baptist, Hooper Farm Road
Methodist, Centre Street at Main
St. Mary's Roman Catholic, Federal Street
St. Paul's Episcopal, 16 Fair Street
Unitarian Universalist, 11 Orange Street
Union Chapel, Siasconset (summer
season only)

Information, General

The Nantucket Information Bureau is one of the busiest spots on the Island during the summer. People working here can answer all your questions about the Island. The office is at 25 Federal Street, off Main Street, and the telephone number is 228-0925 or 228-0926.

The Nantucket Chamber of Commerce, located in the Pacific Building at the foot of Main Street's square, also has helpful answers to general information questions about the Island. It also has a publication which has a lot of helpful information. The telephone number is 228-1700.

Information, Historical

The office of the Nantucket Historical Association is located on Union Street off Main Street. The Association has preserved and continues to maintain fourteen old buildings or exhibits for the visitor. It prints a map and a brochure with information about each building and exhibit. There is a $7.50 admission fee for all the exhibits, or separate fees per exhibit.

The people in the office are most helpful to anyone seeking information about the Island's history. The Association's mailing address is P.O. Box 1016, and the telephone is 228-1894.

Library

The Nantucket Library is housed in the Atheneum at the corner of Federal and Lower India streets. The telephone number is 228-1110.

Newspaper

The Island's only newspaper is the *Nantucket Inquirer and Mirror* which is a weekly. Established in 1821, it has all the interesting Island news and facts about the week's goings-on. It is available on Thursdays for 35¢.

The Hub, on Main Street at the corner of Federal Street, is the popular newspaper store of the Island. Besides selling the *Inquirer and Mirror,* it also has *The New York Times* and *The Boston Globe.*

Public Rest Rooms

When you are wandering through the town of Nantucket, you may want a rest room. Facilities can be found at the Information Bureau on Federal Street, on the waterfront at Children's Beach, and on Straight Wharf. There are also public rest rooms at the public beaches all over the Island.

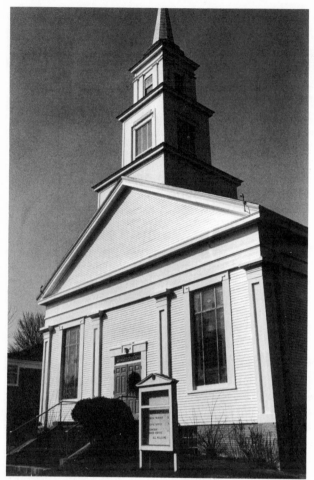

First Baptist Church

*This handsome building on Summer Street was built in
1840, at a time when the Quaker religion was in a
decline (above).*

Methodist Church

*The Methodist Church was built on Centre Street in
1823, and the striking Doric-columned front was
added in 1840 (top right).*

The Hub

*This is the town's popular newspaper store, midway
along the cobblestoned Main Street Square (bottom).*

Public Telephones

You will find pay telephones at the Information Bureau, on the wharves, and on several main streets in town.

Zip Codes

The postal zip code of Nantucket is 02554, and for Siasconset it is 02564.

Leisure Activities

8

Antique Galleries

Three things the visitor to Nantucket hopes to find
— and he won't be disappointed — are good food,
beautiful beaches, and fine antiques. There are
about two dozen antique shops in town. Many of
them specialize in certain things such as scrimshaw
and Sailor's Valentines (those octagonal, wooden
boxes with heart-shaped shell mosaics inside that
sailors brought back from Barbados). Other shops
have Lightship Baskets, China Trade porcelains, or
country furniture. One shop down on Washington
Street has nothing but bird prints and old decoys.

Art Galleries

Like all summer resorts, Nantucket has a wide variety of art galleries that carry everything from modest prints of Island scenes to expensive oil paintings. There are many galleries down along the waterfront as well as some in the center of town.

Art Instruction

There are two places one may take art lessons and they are both open year round. The length of the courses and the subject matter vary from year to year. The Nantucket Island School of Design and The Arts on Wauwinet Road offers lectures, seminars, and college credit courses in drawing, painting, sculpture, printmaking, photography, and others. For more information, call 228-9248.

The Artists' Association on Straight Wharf closes its two galleries during the winter months, but the workshop remains open all year, offering courses in weaving, painting, pottery, and other disciplines. More information is available at 228-0722.

While you're on Nantucket Island, be sure to stop in at the Sailor's Valentine Gallery to see their collection of Sailor's Valentines.

Astronomy

The Loines Observatory of the Maria Mitchell Association is open Wednesday evenings during the summer to the general public. The association also conducts children's classes in astronomy. Friday afternoon seminars are presented by visiting scientists and undergraduate assistants from such institutions as California State Polytechnic University (Cal. Tech.), NASA, and Massachusetts Institute of Technology (M.I.T.). There is also a lecture series of about twenty talks during the summer, again with many distinguished speakers. About half these programs are slanted towards the young audience. The Observatory is on Milk Street Extension and can be phoned at 228-9273.

Beaches

Nantucket beach sand is just right for stretching out, building sandcastles, or walking, for it isn't too fine, nor is it too granular and pebbly. There are beaches on the harbor or Nantucket Sound side of the Island where the waves are very gentle. The beaches on the ocean have waves that average about one to two feet, and sometimes build up to six feet after a storm.

There are three public beaches in town and five public beaches out of town. In town, the Children's Beach on Harbor View Way, just west of the Steamship Dock, has a lifeguard on duty, and food, bath house and rest room facilities. Another good beach for children is the South Beach, on Washington Street next to the shipyard. A lifeguard is on duty, and there are rest room facilities.

Also in town is the Jetties Beach on North Beach Street, along the north shore of the Island, west of Brant Point. This Nantucket Sound beach has lifeguards, rest rooms, bath houses, public tennis courts, and a restaurant. There are beach umbrellas, chairs, towels, Sunfish windsurfers, and Hobie Cats for rent.

Dionis Beach is an out-of-town beach on Nantucket Sound. It is located west of Jetties Beach, along the north shore, about two and a half miles from the center of town. A lifeguard is on duty here, and there are rest room facilities.

Madaket Beach, approximately five and a half miles from town, has ocean surf swimming. The currents are very dangerous around Smith Point and Eel Point here. A lifeguard is on duty.

Cisco Beach, in the Hummock Pond Road area, is a popular area on the Island for surfing. There is a lifeguard, but no other facilities. The beach is approximately four and a half miles from the center of town.

The Surfside Beach on Surfside Road is one of the most popular swimming spots on the Island. There is surf swimming here, under the watchful eyes of the lifeguard. Approximately two and one half miles from town, the beach is reached by direct bus service as well as a bicycle path. A bath house, small snack bar, rest room, and the ever-present bicycle stand make this a convenient place to spend a day.

Codfish Park, the town beach at Siasconset, is approximately seven and a half miles from town. Bus service is provided from town, and there is also a bicycle path. It is surf swimming here and sometimes there is seaweed. A lifeguard is on duty and there are rest room facilities.

M.C. WALLO

The beaches on the Nantucket Sound side of the Island have very gentle waves.

Berry Picking

It has reached the point where there are so few berry bushes left on the Island that the visitor is advised **not** to pick any berries. The same is true for wild grapes. The much touted beach plum is not as prevalent on Nantucket as it is on the Cape, and the huge Cranberry Bog at Gibbs Pond is a private business. However, the cranberry jelly and chutney, as well as honey from the hives alongside the bog, are available in the shops.

Birdwatching

Nantucket is a joy for the birdwatcher. The birds are everywhere in the summer; songbirds inshore, while ducks, geese, terns, egrets, and others haunt the marshes and ponds to nest and feed. Nantucket is right on the migratory path of many birds, so in the winter months Arctic seabirds take refuge in Island waters. During the summer, the Maria Mitchell Association's Natural Science Department sponsors birdwalks three mornings a week which have become increasingly popular. For further details call the Hinchman House at 228-0898.

Boat Rentals and Instruction

Nantucket waters are perfect for sailing or fishing from a rowboat. Boats can be rented from the following businesses. Note that many of them also provide boating instruction.

Erickson's Marine, Commercial Wharf, 228-2045 (instruction also)

Harbor Sail Livery, Washington Street Ext., 228-1757 (instruction also)

Holdgates Boat Rental, 45 Washington Street, 228-9363

Indian Summer Sports, above Young's Bicycle Shop and at Jetties Beach, 228-3632 (instruction also)

Nantucket Sail, Swain's Wharf, 228-4897 (instruction also)

Bowling

For an impossible rainy spell, the bowling alley in mid-Island, just off the Old South Road, will be fun for those who enjoy the sport.

Children's Activities

There are two small crescent-shaped beaches in the town of Nantucket that are perfect for children. One, which is known as the Children's Beach, is adjacent to and directly west of the Steamboat Wharf. The other is known as South Beach and is located on Washington Street. There are lifeguards at both beaches and rest rooms.

When children have had too much sun, there are several other activities provided just for them. The Nantucket Library, the Atheneum on Lower India Street, offers story hour on Saturday mornings. Call 228-1110 for more details.

The Observatory of the Maria Mitchell Association offers astronomy lectures on Tuesday mornings. Its telephone number is 228-9273. The association's Natural Science Museum at the Hinchman House holds nature classes for children. Call 228-0898.

The Chamber Music Center at the Coffin School (228-0525) provides music lessons; the Artist's Association on Straight Wharf (228-0722) gives art lessons; and sailing lessons are available from a number of boat rental companies (see the listings under Boat Rentals and Instruction).

Concerts

The Musical Arts Society gives concerts every Tuesday evening during July and August. Call 228-3735 for more information.

The Arts Council gives Friday evening performances at the Methodist Church from September to June, but does not perform in the summer.

The Chamber Music Center has two choral and instrumental concerts a year, one in the spring and one in the fall. Call the Coffin School (228-0525) for more details.

Band concerts are held every night at 7 p.m. during July and August in the gazebo at Harbor Square down on the waterfront.

Noonday concerts are held every Thursday in July and August at the Unitarian Church at 11 Orange Street, with guest soloists and ensembles.

Evening Entertainment

There are no nightclubs or discos on Nantucket, but the following places do have a piano player or other musicians performing in their bars until closing: the Brotherhood, the Opera House, Chanticleer, the Tavern, the White Elephant, and the Club Car. There is dancing nightly from 9 p.m. to 1 a.m. at the Harbor House.

Check with the various boat rental places if you're interested in an evening sunset sail. The availability of boats changes from season to season.

The Nantucket Lobster Trap prepares clambakes which can be taken to Brant Point or Jetties Beach for an evening picnic. The sunset over Nantucket Sound makes these beaches beautiful in the early evening.

There are lectures, movies, concerts, art gallery shows, and plays on different evenings. All the inns and hotels have a calendar of events.

Fall Foliage

Unlike the wildflowers which should **never** be picked, picking dried grasses in the fall for an arrangement won't hurt the plants. The salt hay and other marsh grasses, brown milkweed pods, bayberry, delicate sea lavendar, and bittersweet make attractive fall bouquets. The cattail which survives best in brackish water around the edges of the salt marshes is the less common, narrow-leafed variety. It has crossbred, as often happens on the Island, and slim, medium, and fat ones can be found. There is

Mitchell's Book Corner is one of many popular stores on Main Street.

LLERY
UDIO

still plenty of wild grape on the Island, and the vines can be cut to make the wreaths, assuming one has permission from the property owner.

Fishing

Fish abound in the shoal waters swirling around the Island, as well as in the calmer harbor and lagoons. Bluefish, flounder, scup, swordfish, Bonita codfish, and black sea bass are the most familiar. For the sports fisherman, bluefish and swordfish are the true game fish and the most sought after. Bluefish not only put up a good fight, they are very plentiful alongshore from May through October. Charter boats are available by the day or half day to go out in the rips to fish, or one can surfcast for the fish along the Island's south and east shores.

In midsummer, swordfish prefer the warm waters of the Gulf Stream which is about sixty to eighty miles southeast of Nantucket. They are scarce, but can be caught — if you are lucky — with a harpoon. They are also caught commercially by long lining (which is just that, a very long line with hooks on it). Years ago, swordfish were caught within ten miles of the Island, but like all species which become very popular, they have become scarce.

The Atlantic Bonita is also another popular game fish for the sportsmen. Large schools of them usually arrive in Nantucket Sound around the first of August and are gone by September. Years ago large catches were made in gill nets all through the month of September.

Fishing for striped bass, which is always done at night, in the fall, and in the cooler water preferred by the fish, has declined in popularity because the fish have become so scarce in recent years. The Madaket area was a favorite spot for bass fishing. Unfortunately, the level of PCB in both the bass and the bluefish has now become a health concern.

The bottomfish — flounder and scup — are found in quiet water, such as Nantucket Harbor, rather than the open ocean. They can be fished for from a rowboat, or a favorite method for young children is to drop a hook and line off a dock, using quahog meat for bait. These fish are good to eat.

The codfish is a winter fish that by June has gone offshore to deeper water. It is as delicious and prevalent in Nantucket waters as the eel, but is far more popular. At the turn of the century and later, eels were often caught through the ice and shipped to New York City, particularly at Christmastime, where the Italians considered them a delicacy. Both the cod and the eel were also salted and exported.

The Island bookstores have various titles that describe all the fish which are found in waters around the Island.

Flight Instruction

Flight instruction is available at the Nantucket Memorial Airport which is located on the south side of the Island, six miles from town. For more information, call 228-0894.

Golf

There are two public, nine-hole golf courses on the Island: the Siasconset Golf Club (257-6596) and the Miacomet Golf Club on Hummock Pond Road (228-9764).

Horseback Riding

Somerset Stables, on Somerset Road off of Vesper Lane, has horses for rent. They have their own trails for horseback riding and beach privileges so one can go riding along the ocean. They also take riders on guided trail rides (228-3358).

Kite Flying

The Nantucket Kiteman on the Old South Wharf has an extraordinary selection of kites in his shop, and the beaches lend themselves beautifully to this popular pastime.

*Nantucket's beaches on the ocean have waves that
average about one to two feet (above).
Fishing is an enjoyable pastime for Nantucket visitors
and residents (top left).
The Somerset Riding Academy has beach privileges so
one can go riding along the ocean (bottom left).*

Lectures

The Maria Mitchell Association (228-0898) has lectures on astronomy, nature, botany, and birds which go on year round. The Kenneth Taylor Gallery on Straight Wharf (228-0722) sponsors lectures on the arts on Monday evenings.

Music Instruction

The Chamber Music Center at the Coffin School on Winter Street has teachers to give lessons, year round, in piano, violin, and other string instruments. For further details, call 228-0525.

Nature and Wildflower Walks

The Maria Mitchell Association's Natural Science Department (228-0898) sponsors nature walks on Thursday afternoons in the summer. Plant walks, which have become increasingly popular, rather than formal botany sessions, take place two mornings a week. There are both nature and plant walks scheduled in the spring and fall, and Friday night lectures during the winter. The department has a pamphlet for sale which is a self-guided walk to Eel Point.

The Gulf Stream, which passes just 200 miles south of Nantucket on its way due northeast to Ireland, accounts for the Island's extraordinary vegetation that is a treasure trove to botanists. A meeting ground for northern and southern plants, unlike any other place in the country, there are over one thousand varieties of plant life on the Island. The prickly pear cactus one associates with the Midwest blooms in July on Coatue not far from the reindeer moss and wintergreen usually found in northern climates. Holly trees and hawthorns thrive in the mild climate. Plants brought over from Europe for their medicinal qualities now grow wild; horehound, catnip, spearmint, peppermint, yarrow, bonsey, and tansy can be found. Scotch broom and heather blanket the moors and the deliciously fragrant wild azalea is found in the swamps. A few plants are unique to the Island, such as the sugar-plum and the red wood lily.

Pony Races

Miacomet Raceway has amateur harness races on Wednesday nights during the summer season. It's a couple of miles from town, and the contests have a delightful country fair air about them.

Shell Collecting

Brant Point and Pocomo are the best places to find shells, though Nantucket doesn't have an exotic collection. The favorite is the lovely, fluted scallop shell, which has been known through history for its designs on fine china and furniture, and as a religious symbol.

Shellfishing

The location of clams, oysters, and mussels won't be included in this book, because of the rapidly increasing number of people visiting Nantucket. This is a business for the native Islanders who, for the most part, earn their living on a seasonal basis. You may enjoy this wonderful New England seafood in many of the fine restaurants on the Island. Restaurants also serve lobster which is so popular that demand sometimes outstrips supply to the point that they have to be shipped in from Maine.

You may, however, fish for the delicious bay scallop which is harvested only in the wintertime. It is the most valuable Island fish, other than the lobster. The season usually begins the first of November and goes until the end of March. There is a heavy fine for anyone harvesting scallops from spring through fall. Both in Nantucket Harbor and out in the shoal water off Tuckernuck Island, scallopers are out in force the first day of the season, dredging the bottom. There is a limit per day for each fisherman. The part you eat is the muscle, although the rest of the scallop is perfectly edible. Most of the scallops are shipped off-Island.

Shopping

Nantucket has become known for the quality of the merchandise in its gift and clothing stores. The handmade sweaters, materials, and clothing at the Nantucket Looms on lower Main Street at the corner of Union Street are very popular. The various shops attractively display country furniture made from antique woods, china, glass, interesting weathervanes, and beautiful needlepoint from Erica Wilson who has a home on the Island. The work of local craftsmen in everything from candles to quilts is featured in many of the stores. There are also the usual number of souvenir shops, particularly along the waterfront.

When you're looking for a good book to read on the beach, you'll want to try Mitchell's Book Corner at 54 Main Street or The Bookworks at 25 Broad Street.

Tennis

The pleasant weather of Nantucket makes it an enjoyable place to play tennis. There are tennis courts at Jetties Beach, on Somerset Road at Miacomet Tennis Courts, and off North Beach Street at Seacliff Tennis Club. Visitors also may play tennis at the private Siasconset Casino between 12:00 and 2:00 p.m., upon paying a fee at the front door.

Theatres

There are three theatres on the Island that show movies. The Dreamland Theatre on South Water Street (unlisted phone number) shows movies through the summer season only. The Siasconset Casino (257-6585), a private tennis club, shows current movies during summer evenings to the public. The Gaslight Theatre on North Union Street (228-4435) is open year round. During the summer, the

Nantucket Historical Documentary Film is shown here several times daily, while current movies are shown in the evenings.

The Theatre Workshop at 2 Twin Street (228-4721) presents plays using amateurs who live on the Island as the actors. These plays are very popular, summer and winter, and are performed at Bennett Hall on Centre Street.

Walking Tours

The best way to become acquainted with the Island is to take at least one (and preferably all) of the three tours of Nantucket that are described in this book.

Tour I: The Center of Town

9

This tour of Nantucket should be done on foot and is designed for those with limited time. You'll find the twisting lanes and alleyways paved in brick and cobblestone have names that reflect global voyages. The houses themselves are usually named after the original owner, a practice which is followed in many New England towns where such things can be easily traced. The Nantucket Historical Association has preserved fourteen old buildings and exhibits for the visitor that are found on these first two tours. There is a flat fee of $7.50 to visit all exhibits, which can be paid at the Peter Folger Museum, or an admission fee is charged at each of the exhibits.

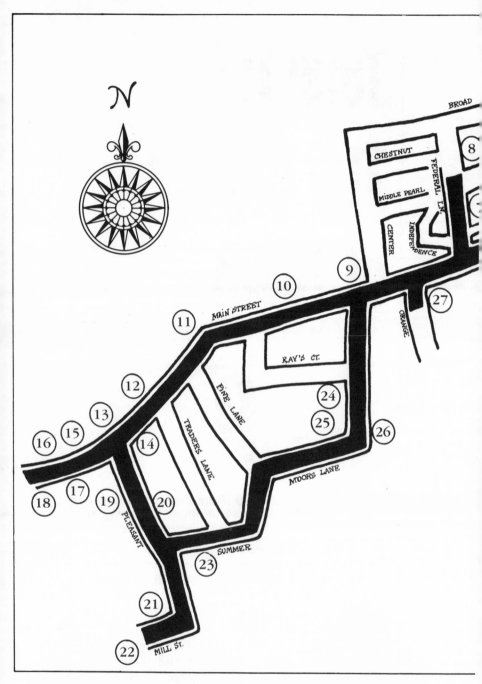

POINTS OF INTEREST: 1. Nantucket Harbor 2. Nantucket Lightship 3. Whaling Museum 4. Peter Foulger Museum 5. Main Street Square 6. Pacific Club 7. St. Mary's Roman Catholic Church 8. Nantucket Atheneum 9. Pacific Bank and Methodist Church 10. John Wendell Barrett House 11. Henry Coffin House and Charles Coffin House 12. Mathew Crosby House 13. The Three Bricks 14. William Hadwen Houses

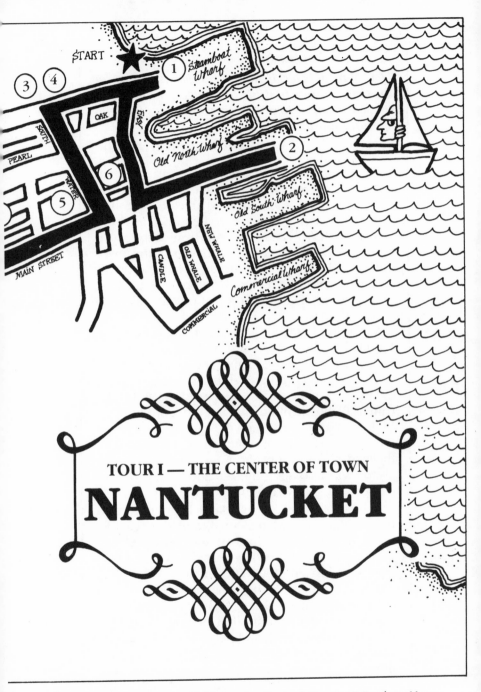

TOUR I — THE CENTER OF TOWN

NANTUCKET

15. Thomas Macy II House 16. Christopher Starbuck House 17. Zaccheus Macy House 18. Richard Gardner House 19. William Crosby House 20. Walter Folger House 21. Moor's End 22. 1800 House 23. Baptist Church 24. Friends Meeting House 25. Fair Street Museum 26. St. Paul's Episcopal Church 27. Unitarian Church (Old South Tower)

1. Nantucket Harbor

"The Nantucketer, he alone resides and riots on the sea; he alone in Bible language, goes down to the sea in ships; to and fro plowing it as his own special plantation . . ."

MOBY DICK Herman Melville

Walking up from the Steamboat Wharf you will come to Easy Street, on your left, which will take you over to the four other wharves on the harborfront. The first one you come to is Old North Wharf which is privately owned. The next street you come to is Dock Street, and just beyond is the lower end of Main Street. Both streets lead right out to Straight Wharf, which is public, along with the next two wharves, Old South and Commercial (also called Swain's).

Mr. Walter Beinecke, Jr., bought, and restored or rebuilt this whole area, preserving the cobblestone mall lined with old gaslights and beautiful shade trees. The weathered-grey shingled cottages out on the piers have the small-paned windows and white trim of all the old buildings; they are reproductions built by Beinecke to retain the special character of the town. Wandering along these wharves with their art galleries, gift shops, and restaurants, the visitor will also see sailboats and motorboats of every size and description tied to the piers.

It was, of course, Nantucket's large, protected harbor that created the town, and the sea that molded her human history and provided her wealth. In the nineteenth century this whole waterfront area looked quite different; it was cluttered, messy, and smelly. In 1828 Daniel Webster was so surprised when he visited Nantucket he later reported in a speech in the U.S. Senate: "Nantucket itself is a very striking and peculiar portion of the National interest. There is a population of eight or nine thousand persons, living here on the sea, adding largely every year to the National wealth by the boldest and most persevering industry."

Mary Cushing Edes in 1835 wrote to her sister, Charlotte Cushing, who lived outside of Boston: "The streets are sandy and they run in every direction. When you go out walking you return with shoes full of dirt, although some of the streets have sidewalks. The houses set any way. Travel over the rutted roads is mostly in a calash, a two wheel open box wagon and standing mostly to soften the jolting. It is good fun once in a while but such exercise is not desireable often. You never saw anything like the place."

In her book *Nantucket Landfall,* Dorothy Blanchard had a more romantic view of the waterfront and wrote of "the odor of whale oil and salt ocean pleasantly shot with the fragrances of Cadiz olives, Sicilian oranges, Smyrna figs, muscatel raisins, Oriental spices and teas . . . " brought in from those protracted whaling voyages to the South Seas, Indian Ocean, and China. With a population of 8,000, or more, and nearly one hundred vessels in the whaling fleet, Nantucket was one of the busiest and wealthiest ports in America.

2. Nantucket Lightship
Straight Wharf

Moored at Straight Wharf is one of the famous Nantucket Lightships. In the mid-nineteenth century lightships were stationed off the south and east ends of the Island to protect the trans-Atlantic maritime traffic from the treacherous shoal waters swirling around Nantucket. The first South Shoal Lightship was stationed 24 miles out at sea in 1856 with a crew of ten who were assigned several months duty at a time.

The duty on these lightships gave birth to a cottage industry that became as important to Nantucket as whaling. Just as the whaler turned to scrimshaw to while away the long dreary hours at sea, some of the men aboard the South Shoal Lightship wove baskets. (For some unknown reason, no baskets were made on the other lightships.)

Nantucket Lightship Baskets

Shown near the Nantucket Lightship are Bill and Judy Sayle's Nantucket Lightship baskets. One is decorated with an ivory shell carved by Charles Sayle, Sr. (top left).

John Wendell Barrett House

One of the town's most elegant homes, this Federal house was built at 72 Main Street by John Wendell Barrett (bottom left).

Pacific Club

The Pacific Club on Lower Main Street was formed by a group of Nantucket shipmasters in 1854. The iron drinking fountain for horses in the foreground was a familiar sight in the days before the "horseless carriage" (right).

By 1905 the South Shoal Lightship was automated, and the men came ashore. The basket making continued, as retired seamen gathered in their workshops to make and sell these baskets to the tourists. The baskets developed in several stages from the loosely woven utilitarian Indian baskets, to heavy-duty farm baskets for carrying wood and produce, to the beautifully made baskets we know today which were the inspiration of José Reyes and the Sayle family.

José Reyes, a Filipino, came to the Island right after World War II to teach Spanish. Unable to find a job, he turned to basket making, and around 1947 he made a basket with a mahogany top for Charlie Sayle's wife. A carver, writer, and veteran of the coastwise schooner trade, Charlie later carved a black ebony whale which his wife suggested they put on the top of the basket. One day they showed it to José who liked the idea so much Charlie began doing some carving for him for the fittings and the top. The second one José made for Mrs. Sayle had five small ivory whales on the top of the basket.

The Lightship baskets immediately became very popular. Today the tradition is carried on by Charlie Sayle's son and daughter-in-law, Bill and Judy Sayle, who have their own shop, and others.

The Lightships became much more famous to the average person for the handbags than for the vitally important duty for which they were established. Fortunately the South Shoal Lightship has become an exhibit of the Nantucket Historical Association and one can go aboard during the summer to see how these men lived and how the vessel was operated. The admission fee is $1.00.

3. *Whaling Museum*
   Broad Street

Return on Easy Street to the head of the Steamboat Wharf and go left one block to the corner of South Beach and Broad Street where you will find two museums on your right that are managed by the

Nantucket Historical Association. The building of the Whaling Museum was originally a candle factory built in 1847. A guided tour by the museum staff explains how the various items on exhibit were used in whaling. There's a replica of the type of brick Try-Works used on the deck of a whaleship to boil down the "liquid gold." Other whaling instruments such as harpoons, lances, bailers, skimmers, and a whaleboat, scrimshaw, and ship models are also on display. And there's a jawbone of a whale which rises two stories giving the visitor some idea of the extraordinary skill it must have taken to harpoon a whale. The admission charge is $2.50.

4. Peter Foulger Museum
Broad Street

The Peter Foulger Museum, next to the Whaling Museum, is a diary of the refinements obtained from the Island's early years. There are antique farm tools, oil paintings, lightship baskets, exquisite porcelains from the China Trade, Nantucket silver, beautiful silks, Oriental rugs, and rare pieces of furniture brought back on the whaleships, as well as a superb maritime library. The museum was established by a member of the Folger family who requested that the old spelling, Foulger, be used for the name. The admission charge is $1.50. It is here that you may purchase the $7.50 ticket to all the Historical Association's exhibits.

5. Main Street Square

Leaving the museums, go straight across the street onto South Water Street and continue until you come to the foot of Main Street.

The center of the town is a very broad, cobblestoned square approximately three blocks long with attractive shops in the old brick buildings lining either side of the street. The old drinking fountain for horses, in the middle of the street at the foot of the square, was moved from upper Main Street to its present location at the turn of the century.

The cobblestones were laid in 1837 to prevent the wheels of wagons, laden with heavy oil casks, from sinking into the sandy streets. They had been brought back as ballast in whaleships when they returned from voyages with little cargo. Granite slabs, used in places as curbstones, were also brought back as ballast.

After the devastating fire in 1846 when hundreds of buildings were destroyed, it was decided to greatly broaden Main Street, and to rebuild with brick and slate to help avoid another such catastrophe. The lower part of the square had been narrow, so the whole square was made rectangular, and marble slabs were set at the street corners as monuments. (Many of these have disappeared.) The brick sidewalks are wide, allowing room for benches, and the familiar, traditional sidewalk and flower carts are always there. The two Pacific buildings face one another at either end of the square; the Pacific Club at the lower end, the bank at the upper, not only adding to the symmetry of this handsome center, but also acting as constant reminders of the town's historic roots.

6. The Pacific Club
Main Street

The Pacific Club at the foot of the square was built by William Rotch, the successful shipowner whose vessels *Beaver* and *Dartmouth* were involved in the famous Boston Tea Party; who was famous for his defense of the black sailor, Boston; and whose ship *Bedford* was the first American vessel to enter a British port after the Revolution. Rotch designed the building as a warehouse for oil and candles used in direct trade with London. The building also was used as a customs house. In 1859 a group of former whaling shipmasters who had sailed the Pacific formed a club and bought the building. Here they gathered to spin yarns of a lifetime at sea, and play cribbage and whist. Over a century old, the club is still active.

7. *St. Mary's Roman Catholic Church*
Federal Street

Walking up Main Street, turn right on Federal Street. A short distance down on your right is St. Mary's Roman Catholic Church. Catholicism came late to Nantucket and services first began in the Old Town Hall in 1849. In 1858, Harmony Hall on Federal Street was consecrated as St. Mary's Church. Then in 1896 the old building was removed and replaced by the present structure.

8. *Nantucket Atheneum*
Lower India Street

Farther along, at the corner of Federal and Lower India streets, is the Atheneum, a very handsome Greek Revival building, which is the Nantucket Library. The original library was completely destroyed in the terrible fire of 1846 when many very valuable old books were lost. It was rebuilt within six months and no expense was spared which was extraordinary considering the terrible plight of the town at the time.

9. *Pacific Bank and The Methodist Church*
Main Street

Return to Main Street and up at the head of the square five streets come together (Fair, Orange, Centre, Liberty and Main, with a few steps between). The Pacific National Bank, which faces the Pacific Club and also reminds the visitor of the importance of the Pacific in Nantucket's history, was built in 1818 of imported pressed brick. Its solid exterior is matched by its solvent interior for it came through the great fire of 1846 and the 1929 stock market crash unscathed!

Next to the bank is the United Methodist Church which was built in 1823 just as Nantucket was forging into its golden era and the Quaker faith was beginning to wane. The Doric-columned front was added in 1840.

Across the Main Street side of the Pacific Bank is Murray's clothing store. It was here that Rowland Macy gave up storekeeping with his father, went whaling, became a "forty-niner," and later opened his own department store in New York City — R.H. Macy & Co.

Main Street Houses

"Never a Captain grizzled and gray Now climbs to the house-top walk, Pipe and spyglass are put away: But the wise ones sometimes talk Of the pleasant ghosts that are peering still Through the glasses out to sea Thinking back to the lure of the ships And the life that used to be."

THE WALK Mary Starbuck

On upper Main Street and Pleasant Street are some very old houses, and most of the elegant mansions built with whaling money. A good many of these houses are now owned by summer residents.

As you wander on up Main Street look up and down — up to the rooftops of these beautiful houses as the various architectural features are noted, and down, underfoot, at the cobblestone, lovely old small pink brick in places, and the granite slabs on the curbs.

10. John Wendell Barrett House
72 Main Street

The white, clapboard Federal house at 72 Main Street was built by John Wendell Barrett, a successful whale oil merchant and president of the Pacific Bank. Notice the handsome balustrade trim along the edge of the roof, higher than usual foundation, portico over the front, enclosed cupola, and glassed sidelights on either side of the six-panel door.

Barrett's wife, Lydia, was a stalwart lady, indeed, and when the fire of 1846 was approaching her house, the firemen asked her to leave so they could dynamite the house to try to stop the blaze. She refused, and told them they would have to blow her up too. Fortunately for all, there was a slight shift in the wind, and the blazing inferno did not reach the house.

11. Henry Coffin House & Charles Coffin House
75 and 78 Main Street

Farther up the street, facing one another, are the brick, handsome, Georgian-style, Coffin brothers' houses built in the early 1830's. Both men had inherited wealth and whaleships from their father. The structures are identical except that Charles, a Quaker, had sober brownstone trim around his front door and a plain walk on the roof, while Henry, who wasn't a Quaker, preferred more elegant white marble trim around his front door and a cupola. The brothers owned the whaleship *Constitution,* which was one of the first ships to use the camel to get over the bar and out of Nantucket Harbor.

Both men were very civic minded and not only were they responsible for planting the elm trees on Main Street in 1851, but they also imported 30,000 pine trees, which they planted in the treeless outlying areas of the Island. Charles and a friend, David Joy, in 1836 gave to the town the building which was the first Nantucket Library.

12. Mathew Crosby House
90 Main Street

The first owner of this handsome Federal house was a successful whaler and later a shipowner and merchant. Built in 1829, the building is graced with an exceedingly handsome fan over the six-panel front door. The door's sterling silver knocker, doorknob, and nameplate display a certain elegance found in many of these larger homes. The structure is perfectly proportioned, with a handsome balustrade trim on the roof, two chimneys set in from the side walls, and double steps with a gracefully curving handrail leading up to the front door.

13. The Three Bricks
93, 95 and 97 Main Street

Possibly the most famous houses in Nantucket, these three identical Georgian brick mansions were built between 1836 and 1838 by Joseph Starbuck for his three sons William, Mathew, and George. Patriarch of the Starbuck clan, Joseph had made millions with his whaleships and built these three handsome houses for $54,000, but kept the title to the properties to make sure his sons would stay in the family business. Starbuck also built a whaleship called *Three Brothers* which returned to Nantucket in 1859 after a five-year voyage with 6,000 barrels of oil, both feats being record making.

The houses are called East Brick, Middle Brick, and West Brick. They have identical porticos with black wrought iron fences, and their four chimneys are flush with the outside walls.

14. William Hadwen Houses
94 and 96 Main Street

Joseph Starbuck also had three daughters, and they lived at 92, 96, and 100 Main Street, the area being a regular compound of wealthy merchants and their families. One of Joseph's daughters married William Hadwen, a native of Newport, Rhode Island, who came to the Island and worked as a silversmith. Later he operated the candle factory that is now the Whaling Museum. He engaged Frederick Brown Coleman, architect of the Baptist Church, to build his Greek Revival mansion, and the one next door for his niece and adopted daughter, Mrs. George (Mary G. Swain) Wright.

The houses are nearly identical although the columns on Number 94 are reputed to be copied from the portico of the "Tower Of Winds" in Athens. A second floor ballroom had a specially sprung dance floor and a rooftop dome which could be opened to the stars. Number 96, now owned by the Historical Association, is the only mansion open to the public. Its interior gives the visitor an understanding of how Nantucket's wealthy residents lived and furnished their homes. Admission fee is $1.50 and the house is open every day from June through October.

Staircase in the Hadwen House

This magnificent circular staircase is in the Greek Revival Hadwen House on Main Street.

15. *Thomas Macy II House*
99 Main Street

What many consider the handsomest doorway in Nantucket adorns this white clapboard house which was built in 1770, and added onto in 1827. One of the earliest houses to show a big change from the stark simple lines of the Quaker houses, this one was originally a typical four-bay (window) house which Macy's father-in-law had purchased for $432. A former blacksmith, Macy became a successful shareholder in several whaling ships, and in the course of remodeling and enlarging his house, he kept the proportions beautifully in balance. He included many rather than a few of the adornments beginning to appear on Nantucket houses, and instead of looking cluttered, it is striking.

Macy converted the house to a two-chimney residence with a central hall. The porch railing curves out from the door to the street and makes the front fence. The front door itself is topped by a blind (wooden rather than glass) fan; there are fluted columns on either side of the door, then the sidelights, or glass windows on either side of the door. An unusual feature is the second story window over the front door which also has sidelights. Notice the well-proportioned roof walk which is not out of proportion although it runs almost the full length of the roof.

16. Christopher Starbuck House
105 Main Street

While the Coffins and Starbucks accounted for thirteen of Main Street's handsome houses between them, the Macys were not far behind with five homes in the area to their credit (Numbers 77, 86, 89, 99, and 107).

A few houses were moved to this area from the original Sherburne settlement. The eastern section of this house is thought to have been built in 1690 in Sherburne, while the western half dates from about 1715. It is a typical Nantucket lean-to with many features of the second stage in the development of Island houses. It has twelve-over-twelve windows and a very plain door with a five-pane light over it.

17. Zaccheus Macy House
107 Main Street

Typical of many Nantucket houses built at this time, this 1748 silvery grey shingled five-bay house has twelve-over-twelve windows, very plain front door, and a picket fence. The fence gives an aesthetic touch as it ties one building to another, although it was built originally for the very practical purpose of keeping animals out. The house was built by the grandson of Thomas Macy, the Island's first settler. Although Zaccheus was a prominent merchant and boat builder, he is best remembered for his medical ability to set broken bones, a favorite hobby which, fortunately for his patients, he had studied in his youth. It is estimated that he set more than 2,000 in his lifetime, all free of charge. He was extremely well liked, a staunch friend of the Indians, and a noted historian.

M.C. WALLO

117

Thomas Macy Doorway

Many people consider the doorway on the Thomas Macy house at 99 Main Street to be the most handsome one in Nantucket.

118

18. Richard Gardner House
139 Main Street

Richard Gardner's father came to the Island in 1666, and this shingled, second generation house (meaning it was built by the son of an original settler) is dated around 1690. It is an excellent example of a very early house. With its heavy door with long, black, iron hinges, heavy beams, walls insulated with mud and wattle, oblong, diamond-shaped pane windows, and massive off-center chimney, it has many of the characteristics of a medieval cottage.

19. William Crosby House
1 Pleasant Street

You are now at the Civil War Monument which is in the middle of the street. Turn back towards town, on Main Street, and take your first right onto Pleasant Street. The handsome Greek Revival home on the corner, built in 1837, has a high foundation, large French windows, double parlors, silver doorknobs, marble mantels, and handblocked wallpaper.

Crosby was a prosperous young whaling merchant, married to the daughter of whaling Captain Seth Pinkham, when he had the house built. Known for their attractive social gatherings, the Crosbys introduced frozen mousse to their friends and imported the first Chickering piano with which to

Richard Gardner House
The Richard Gardner House at 139 Main Street is one of the Island's oldest surviving houses (top).
Walter Folger House
Walter Folger always lived in this simple, but handsome, typical four-bay Quaker house at 8 Pleasant Street (middle).
Moor's End
This beautiful Georgian brick mansion with its serpentine brick wall enclosing a garden is thought to be Nantucket's most magnificent house. It is located at 19 Pleasant Street (bottom).

entertain their friends. Unfortunately this lifestyle was not to last, for the fire of 1838 which swept the wharf destroyed a huge amount of oil Crosby had stored, and he suffered heavy losses. He survived this, only to have almost all of his holdings go up in flames in the fire of 1846, and the Crosbys were forced to sell their house.

20. *Walter Folger House*
8 Pleasant Street

The owner of this unpretentious house was the Island's genius in the early nineteenth century. Walter Folger was a mathematician, state senator, U.S. congressman, as well as a fine mechanic and inventor of an astronomical clock, now displayed in the Foulger Museum. This extraordinary clock not only indicated the seconds, minutes, and hours of the day, and the days of the month, but also showed the phases of the moon, the positions of the sun, and the height of the tide in Nantucket Harbor! A self-taught lawyer, teacher and historian, Walter also studied medicine, learned French in order to study the European philosophers and scientists, and learned astronomy from a French treatise on the subject brought to the Island by a shipwrecked French sailor. His telescope was one of the finest, and he managed to discover spots on Venus other recognized scientists had missed. He also, at one time, had a successful factory for spinning and weaving cotton and wool. Walter was considered as "odd as huckleberry chowder," which isn't surprising as his crowded mind was undoubtedly always distracted from life's mundane things.

Other outstanding members of this family included Abiah, Benjamin Franklin's mother; Charles, a noted New York lawyer who ran against Grover Cleveland for governor of New York; Peter, one of the ablest of the original settlers; and James A. Folger who went to the West Coast and founded the Folger Coffee Company.

21. Moor's End
19 Pleasant Street

This enormous Georgian brick mansion at the corner of Mill Street is considered by many to be Nantucket's most magnificent house. Built between 1829 and 1834 by Jared Coffin who had acquired a fortune through his partnership in three successful whaleships, it has the grandeur of an English manor house. It is famous for its massive brick-walled garden and whaling murals on the dining room walls. Despite its elegance, the house did not satisfy Coffin's wife who wanted to be closer to town, so he built the three-story Jared Coffin House, at the corner of Broad and Centre Streets. Moor's End was sold and resold several times before 1873 when Jared Gardner bought it at auction for $2,350!

22. 1800 House
Mill Street

A short trip up Mill Street takes you to the 1800 house, another Historical Association exhibit that is open to the public. Its furnishings represent a typical Nantucket home as it appeared in the early whaling days. The central chimney with six flues and beehive oven, huge beams, keeping room, borning room, and spinning room convey the way of life for the average Islander at that time in history. The charming old-fashioned herb garden of this former sheriff's home completes the setting. The admission is $1.00, and the house is open daily.

23. Baptist Church
Summer Street and Trader's Lane

Return to Moor's End on Pleasant Street and turn back towards Main Street. Your second right is Summer Street and the Baptist Church is on your left. This handsome building with a graceful spire was built in 1840, further evidence of the decline of the Quaker religion at that time.

24. *Friends Meeting House*
   Fair Street

If you stay on Summer Street and turn left when it dead ends into Pine Street, you will be heading back towards Main Street. A right turn on Moors Lane takes you over to Fair Street. Turn left on Fair Street and go one block to the Friends Meeting House. Built in 1846, this stark, grey, rectangular building is the only remaining Quaker meeting-house left on the Island. Meetings, open to the public, are still held in this building in the summer months.

25. *Fair Street Museum*
   Fair Street

Next to the Meeting House is the Fair Street Museum, another Historical Association exhibit, with a $1.00 admission fee.

The artists John Singleton Copley, Gilbert Stuart, Childe Hassam, Eastman Johnson, Theodore Robinson, as well as Tony Sarg all visited and painted Nantucket. The Fair Museum has become Nantucket's art museum and the growing collection is impressive. It not only includes work by some of the above well-known names, but also interesting primitives by unknown artists.

Tony Sarg first visited the Island in 1920 with a group of artists, and came back for the next twenty summers. He did illustrations for *The Saturday Evening Post,* his own books, and not only produced the famous Macy's Thanksgiving Day Parade, but introduced the huge balloons. Nantucket was, of course, one of his favorite subjects, and a lot of his work may be seen at the museum. His daughter still lives on the Island.

26. *St. Paul's Episcopal Church*
   Fair Street

The Island's first Episcopal Church, a wooden structure built in 1838 on Broad Street, was destroyed in the great fire. This church building, diagonally

123

The Town Crier, 1892

*A self-appointed Town Crier, Billy Clark picked up his
news flashes from the Old South Tower where he
watched for incoming ships, fires, or any other unusual
activity.*

across the street from the Fair Street Museum, was built in 1902 and is noted for its Tiffany windows.

27. *Unitarian Church or Old South Tower*
   Orange Street

Continue along Fair Street until you reach Main Street, turn right and then take your first right onto Orange Street. Over a hundred year period this street, with its fine view of the harbor, was the home of 126 whaling captains. Directly on your right is the Old South Tower which was built in 1809. Although it was originally a Congregational Church, the parishioners gradually became more liberal and embraced Unitarianism. Pew ownership was bought, sold, and auctioned like real estate. The first town clock was placed in the tower in 1823 following the installation of a bell in 1815. It has rung continuously for over 150 years three times a day — at 7 a.m., 12 noon, and 9 p.m. (which was, at one time, the curfew hour). Each time it strikes 52 times, which might have something to do with the weeks in a year, although the reason for this is lost to history.

The tower was also very useful to Billy Clark, the most colorful of Nantucket's many town criers. He would climb the tower to scan the water for an incoming steamer, and if he saw one, he'd thrust his tin horn through the slats of the belfry to announce the vessel's arrival. Then he'd hurry on down to the waterfront to see what news he could pick up. Tooting his horn and ringing his bell to attract attention, he'd wander the streets calling out the latest news items from the mainland, as well as the coming events in town and the latest sales in the local stores. He once announced President Garfield's assassination and a party at the new roller-skating rink all in the same sentence!

This is the last stop on Tour 1. Return to Main Street.

Tour II: The Outskirts of Town

10

If you have the time, this tour covers the interesting landmarks and Historical Association exhibits on the fringes of town. These can be reached by a long, but very worthwhile walk, or by bike or car.

1. Jared Coffin House and
Captain George Pollard House
Corner of Centre and Broad Streets

Next to the Pacific Bank on upper Main Street, turn right onto Centre Street. Three blocks over, where Centre meets Broad Street, is the Jared Coffin House which has been an inn almost from its con-

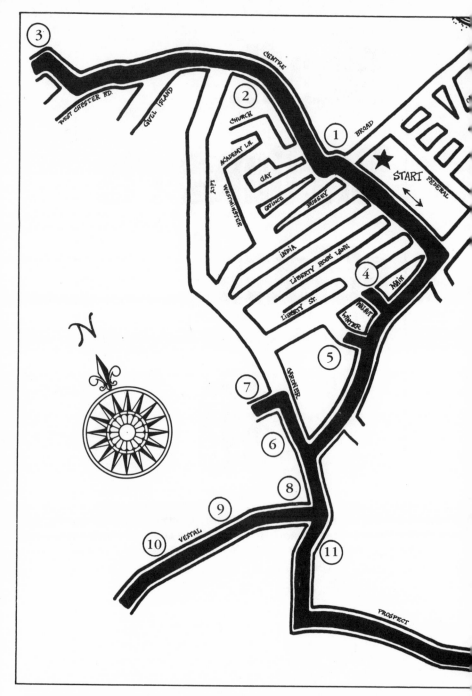

POINTS OF INTEREST: 1. Jared Coffin House and Captain George Pollard House
2. Congregational Church and Old North Vestry 3. Jethro Coffin House 4. Nathaniel
Macy House 5. Sir Isaac Coffin School 6. Old Fire Hose Cart House 7. Greater

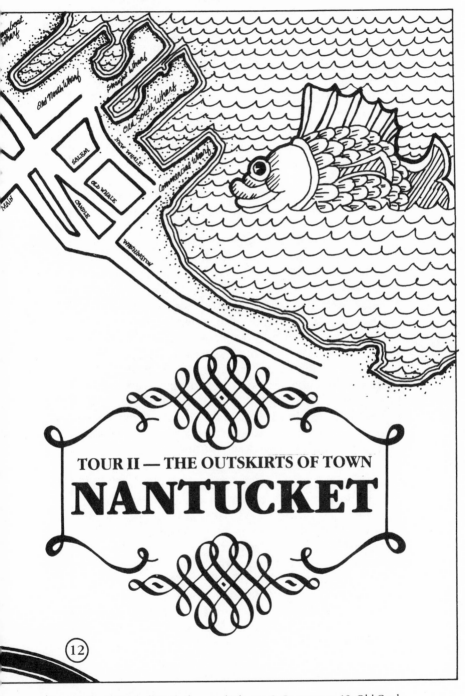

TOUR II — THE OUTSKIRTS OF TOWN
NANTUCKET

struction in 1845. Jared Coffin had built this three-story house (one of the few on the Island) for his wife who had disliked the magnificent Moor's End mansion that he had built for her. His wife was still dissatisfied, and the following year the Coffins moved to Boston. Built of English brick with a Welsh slate roof, and furnished with lovely antiques, the Coffin house is a well-known Nantucket landmark.

Diagonally across the street from the Coffin house is the Seven Seas Gift Shop which was Captain George Pollard's former home. There are many dramatic stories of tragedy and success in whaling, but none surpasses the story of Captain Pollard and his whaleship *Essex* which was rammed and sunk by a whale in 1820. The crew took to their open whaleboats and drifted across the Pacific Ocean for three months. Only eight of the original twenty men survived by eating the flesh of their comrades. In such instances, usually the victim was chosen by drawing straws, or the equivalent, although the cabin boy was often the first to go. In this case, the cabin boy was Captain Pollard's nephew, and they ate him first. Captain Pollard went to sea again, only to be shipwrecked once again. He finally gave it up and settled down for good on the Island, becoming a night watchman.

It was the tragic story of Captain Pollard and his ship, the *Essex,* which Herman Melville heard about in New Bedford and used as the basis for his famous novel, *Moby Dick.* A year after finishing the book, Melville made his first visit to Nantucket. He was walking up Centre Street with a friend towards the Coffin house when he noticed through the thick fog a man coming out of the Pollard house with a watchman's lantern. Pollard raised the lantern as he moved down the steps and Melville caught a glimpse of the old man's face.

"Who is that man?" he asked his companion, and he must have been quite overwhelmed to realize he was looking at Ahab's ghost. Later, Melville re-

marked on this dramatic encounter: "To the Islanders he was a nobody, but to me, the most impressive
man, the most wholly unassuming — even humble
that I ever encountered."

2. Congregational Church and Old North Vestry
62 Centre Street

Continue on Centre Street a few more blocks, and
on your left is the huge, handsome, Gothic Congregational Church built with whaling money in 1834.
The "trompe l'oeil" painting, and huge brass chan-
delier, seven feet wide and over 600 pounds in
weight, enhance this striking building. Behind the
church is the old vestry built in 1725. A small fee is
now charged for the visitor to go up in the church
tower for a spectacular view of the town.

3. Oldest House or Jethro Coffin House
Sunset Hill

Continue on Centre Street out of town, bearing to
the left on Centre, which turns into West Chester,
until you come to Sunset Hill Lane on your right,
and the Jethro Coffin house. It was built in 1686, and
historians debate whether or not it's the oldest
house on the Island. The house was a wedding
present for Jethro Coffin and his bride, Mary
Gardner, from their fathers. The timbers for the
house came from land in New Hampshire belonging to Jethro's father.

The house is a perfect example of a seventeenth-
century house. The prominent features in this
handsome building are the steep shed roof, heavy,
roughhewn hinged door, massive beams, small, diamond-shaped windows, "Indian closet," and a
huge center chimney with a horseshoe design on
the front. There have been many theories about this
design on the chimney. Some believe it might have
been an antiwitch device as the house was built at
the same time as the Salem witch hunts; others
think it might have been symbolic of the union of
two principal families of the full-share and half-

Jethro Coffin House
The Jethro Coffin House on Sunset Hill was built in 1686 and is the oldest house on Nantucket Island (top left).

Maria Mitchell Birthplace and Observatory
The Maria Mitchell Association includes the Loines Observatory, the Maria Mitchell birthplace, and a library, all on Vestal Street (middle left).

The Old Gaol
For two centuries there weren't too many occupants in the old jail on Vestal Street. The prisoners were allowed to go home at night (bottom left).

Civil War Monument
The Civil War Monument on Upper Main Street lists the names of 69 Nantucket men who died in the Civil War (below).

share factions; and then there is the horseshoe as a good luck symbol, although this one is upside down. The house is a Historical Association exhibit and the admission fee is 50¢.

4. *Nathaniel Macy House or Christian House*
Walnut Lane

Returning to the center of town, go to the top of Main Street's square by the bank and continue up Main Street one block. Turn right onto Walnut Lane and at the corner of Liberty is this 1723 house built by Nathaniel Macy, the grandson of the first white settler. This five-bay (window) house has the stark simplicity of many Quaker houses. The interior with its huge fireplaces, primitive cooking utensils, and early eighteenth-century country furniture is well worth a visit. The house is now a Historical Association exhibit and the admission fee is $1.00.

5. *Sir Isaac Coffin School*
Winter Street

Return to Main Street, turn right, and take the next right at Winter Street. A short distance on the left is the Isaac Coffin School. Sir Isaac was raised in Boston, served in the British Royal Navy, and remained a Loyalist during the Revolution. However, he was always an independent Nantucketer at heart. He was a direct descendant of Tristram Coffin. After Sir Isaac retired and moved to Nantucket, he wanted to contribute something of lasting value to the Island. He had no children of his own, but was persuaded to found a school for Coffin children, of whom there were a great many. Nantucket had no public education in those days, only Cent Schools. Parents paid a penny a day to have a child attend classes in one of several homes to learn reading and writing. The first Coffin School was founded on Fair Street, before this handsome brick building with its Doric columns was erected in 1852.

6. Old Fire Hose Cart House
Gardner Street

Return to Main Street, pass the Civil War Monument, and go right on Gardner Street. A short distance ahead on your left is a small building housing some of the earliest firefighting equipment including a hand pumper and some handsome old leather fire buckets.

7. Greater Light
Howard Street

Just beyond the Old Fire House on the left is Howard Street. Here is an old converted barn, named the Greater Light, which is the most unusual exhibit of the Historical Association. The decorative arts in the house are not just Early American or China Trade, but rather a broad collection from Italy, Europe, and the Near East. There is an attractive brick patio, sunken yard and basement dining room. It's closed Sundays and Mondays and the admission charge is $1.00.

8. Maria Mitchell Birthplace and Library
Vestal Street

Return again to the Civil War Monument and go up Milk Street, turning right into Vestal Street. Here on your right is the birthplace, library and observatory of Maria Mitchell, a truly unusual Nantucket lady. Her father, William Mitchell, was a teacher, mathematician, astronomer, and bank cashier. Maria often helped him in "rating" chronometers for shipmasters and making observations of the stars with his telescope.

One fall evening in 1849 while scanning the heavens from her father's small observatory on the roof of the Pacific Bank, Maria discovered a comet. It became known to the outside world, and for her discovery, and other work, she was later awarded a gold medal from the King of Denmark. Although her education had been limited to Nantucket schools, Maria became a Professor of Astronomy at

Vassar College for the second half of the nineteenth century. She became the first woman member of the American Academy of Arts and Sciences and the recipient of many honors. (It's not surprising that she was related to the brilliant Folger family.) Although her father had never attended college, this remarkable man became an overseer at Harvard College.

134

EDWARD JENNER

The Old Mill
The Old Mill on South Mill Street was built in 1746 and is still in use.

Maria's descendants founded the Maria Mitchell Association in her honor. It includes the Loines Observatory, the Maria Mitchell birthplace, a library, and the Natural Science Center at the Hinchman House (Maria's family's first house). The Loines Observatory on Milk Street Extension (on the way to Hummock Pond Road) is open to the public every Wednesday night during the summer.

9. Cooperage
Vestal Street

Farther along Vestal Street on the left is the remaining cooperage on the Island. When whaling was in its prime, there were many, many shops like this, where large and small whale oil casks were made. The wood from the tupelo trees that grow on the Island was very hard and good for making bungs to plug up the barrels.

10. Old Gaol
Vestal Street

Continuing along Vestal Street you'll see the old jail on your right. Constructed of oak logs bolted with iron, sheathed with pine and shingled, the building has four cells with iron bars on the small windows. Two of the cells have fireplaces, and one is sheathed on the inside with iron for the more dangerous criminals, although in two centuries of Island history, there were seldom any prisoners.

11. Hinchman House
7 Milk Street

Backtrack to Milk Street, bear right, and at the corner of Green Street is the natural science museum run by the Maria Mitchell Foundation. There are displays of the Island's flora and fauna in this handsome early nineteenth-century house. The museum sponsors nature and bird walks, as well as seminars and workshops for adults and children.

12. Old Mill
South Mill Street

At the intersection of Milk Street and New Mill Street, go up New Mill one block to Prospect Street and continue along until you come to the junction of South Mill Street. The Old Mill that stands here was built in 1746 and is one of the oldest, if not the oldest, mills in the country. In continuous use since it was built in 1746, the mill is operated entirely by wind power. The original wooden machinery and millstone are still in good working condition, and corn milled on-site is sold at the mill during the summer. There were once four mills in this elevated area, and when Nantucket was caught up in two wars, the mills were used also for signaling ships offshore that were attempting to come into Nantucket Harbor. A Historical Association exhibit, the mill's admission fee is 50¢.

Cemeteries

For those interested in looking at old gravestones, there are five cemeteries in this southwest side of town. The Friends Cemetery is at the junction of Madaket Road and Quaker Road by Caton Circle. The stones here are recent, as Nantucket history goes, because for 150 years, Quaker tradition forbid any headstones. Those you see in the northeastern section date from the final decades of Quakers on Nantucket.

A half mile beyond this is the Abiah Folger Franklin boulder and plaque in memory of Benjamin Franklin's mother who was born near this site. The Prospect Hill Cemetery is bounded by Hummock Pond Road, Cato Lane and Milk Street Extension. The Old South Cemetery, with many very early gravestones, is next to Cyrus Pierce School on Sparks Avenue. The black cemetery is behind the Cottage Hospital, and St. Mary's Roman Catholic Cemetery borders Prospect Street. On the far side of the Quaker Cemetery, at the corner of New Lane

and West Chester Extension, is the Old North Burying Ground which also has some very old headstones.

Tour III: The Outlying Areas

11

These areas out from the town of Nantucket contain little pockets of settlements along the Island's perimeter, both on the harbor side as well as the eastern and southern shores of the Island. There are fingerlike coves reaching in from the sea that are fringed with green ribbons of marsh to provide small harbors in several places along the south shore. The low, rolling moors are dotted with weathered grey shingled houses with winding, narrow dirt roads crisscrossing the area. There are paved roads to all the principal settlements.

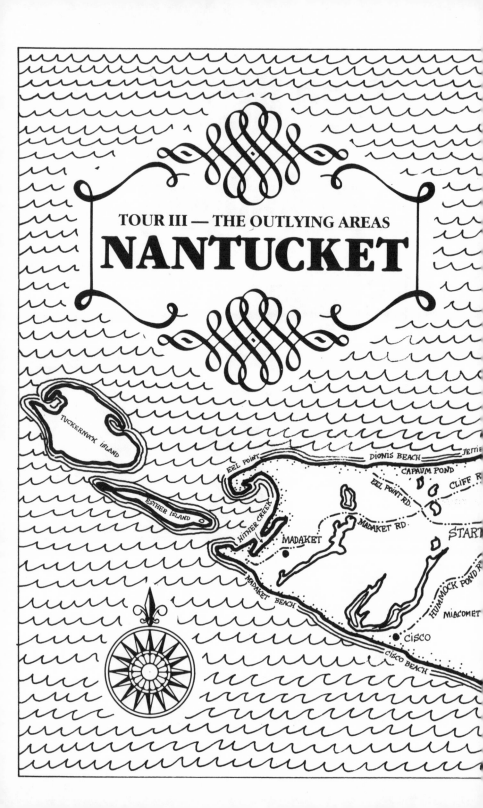

TOUR III — THE OUTLYING AREAS
NANTUCKET

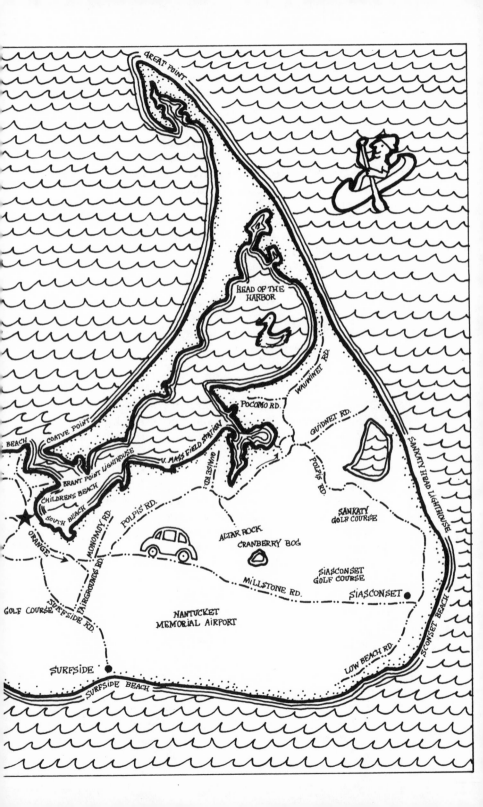

The large, open areas were made possible by the tireless work of many to conserve as much property as possible. Now one-third of Nantucket is protected by private, state or federal organizations to remain forever wild. These large tracts of land help to maintain the delicate balance of natural forces and are critical to the Island's survival as opposed to the massive construction and building that goes on elsewhere.

The low-growing vegetation — bright yellow Scotch broom, bayberry, beach plum, grape, heather, huckleberry, bearberry — and hundreds of wildflowers blanket these areas. So far, no squirrel, chipmunk, racoon, fox, weasel, skunk, porcupine or muskrat has found its way to the Island, although deer, pheasant and cottontail rabbits abound and can be seen on nature walks. Birds of all kinds are everywhere. ·

Monomoy

The tour begins in a clockwise direction, taking Orange Street which is a left turn off Main Street, four blocks up from the foot of the town square at the Pacific Club. Orange Street leads out to a rotary with signs pointing to Siasconset (always called 'Sconset) and Polpis. Bear left on this road, and follow it to Monomoy Road on the left. Turn here, and after a short distance it dead ends at a cluster of houses east of the town of Nantucket. You will have a fine view across the harbor to the town.

Residents living here in these handsome grey shingled houses belong to some of the oldest summer families, along with those in the Cliff area near Jetties Beach. They acquired summer homes here before World War I, while the next wave of summer residents bought in town after World War II.

While you're touring the outlying areas of the Island, be sure to go down to the beaches to appreciate the ocean.

Life Saving Museum
Polpis Road

Return to 'Sconset road, bear left and left again onto Polpis Road. Two miles farther along is the Life Saving Museum, a replica of the first Life Saving Station on Nantucket which was built at Surfside in 1874. Picture if you can this crescent-shaped dollop of land in the Atlantic, which Daniel Webster called that "city in the sea," with shifting sands and currents swirling all around it. To protect or rescue those manning the hundreds of vessels sailing in the area, there were the Lightships positioned offshore as well as "humane" houses at the most vulnerable points around the Island's shores. Here, men would be on the lookout for vessels in distress, and there were many of them. Finally they built lifesaving stations at strategic points around the Island.

The museum has two early lifesaving boats, a breeches buoy, quarterboards, lightship displays, and other equipment used by the heroic men who put out in any weather to rescue survivors of wrecked vessels.

Field Station
University of Massachusetts

Just a short distance beyond the museum, on the left, is the road into the University of Massachusetts' Nantucket Field Station. The Field Station serves as a base for presentation of undergraduate and graduate courses in the natural sciences (field biology, geology, and anthropology) and in the arts and humanities. Courses are offered year round and are open to Nantucket residents as well as mainland students. The Field Station also supports research by senior scientists and scholars from many educational and research institutions. In addition, the Station hosts professional conferences on a variety of topics, and attempts to respond to questions from the public on natural history matters. Although the station has no public exhibits or facilities, and is not open to the public, interested persons may call for an appointment to visit the station. The telephone number is (617) 228-9475. Dr. Wesley N. Tiffney is the director.

Quaise
Quaise Road

Continuing on towards Polpis, the area on your left is Quaise which is about midway along Nantucket Harbor. The Quaise Road is sandy and difficult for a bike or moped, and there is little to see except some private houses. But historically, it is worth noting the area that Thomas Mayhew kept when he sold the rest of the Island to the nine original purchasers. It was once the site of an insane asylum that burned to the ground, and also the home of Keziah Coffin, a devout Loyalist. During the Revolution she carried on a monopoly in trade between Nantucket and New York under the protection of the British Navy when the Americans were prohibiting exports to the Island. A very shrewd and independent woman, Keziah was thoroughly disliked, although Nantucketers were totally dependent on the merchandise she had for sale. After the war, residents joined forces to bring about the collapse of her vast real estate holdings.

Altar Rock

Just opposite the dirt road into Quaise is a dirt road leading to Altar Rock, 90 feet above sea level and the highest point on the Island. It is a very short distance off the main road and one can walk a bike in easily. On a summer day, the view from here of the green, flower-splashed moors, the deep blue of the sea, and the silhouette of the town against a clear sky is well worth the stop.

Polpis

Continue on Polpis Road. In a short distance, there is a rough dirt road leading into Polpis Harbor, but the road is hard to ride on, and there are only private homes on it. In the seventeenth century Polpis was the most successful farming community on the Island. It was also the site of fulling mills where sheep's wool was processed into cloth. Peat digging for fuel was carried on in this area, as well as salt making. This was done by evaporating seawater in

146

Great Point Light
The 166-year-old Great Point Lighthouse was demolished by a storm in March, 1984.

large vats. The salt was not only used for regular cooking, but also to preserve fish. The peaty bottoms of former ponds in the area now nourish beech, maple, oak, and the oriental-looking tupelo trees, as well as ferns, holly, and sassafras.

Nantucket Island School Of Design
Wauwinet Road

Located in an old dairy barn near the junction of the Polpis and Wauwinet roads, is the School of Design. Open year round, it grants graduate and undergraduate credit courses through the Massachusetts College of Art.

Pocomo
Pocomo Road

Continuing on towards Wauwinet, go left on the Pocomo Road which is paved for quite some distance before it becomes a hard to manage dirt road. From the paved road you can get a fine view of the upper part of Nantucket Harbor. A century ago a favorite pastime of visitors to Nantucket was to take a catboat from the town to Pocomo or Wauwinet for "bathing" — one never used the term "swimming" in those days — and a noon picnic. The Pocomo beach, with its crystal clear water and gentle, sandy beach was a favorite spot for years.

Wauwinet
Wauwinet Road

Return to the main road, go left, and in a short distance you'll come to a halt at an information booth. Unless you have a jeep and a permit to explore the area or a house just beyond the hotel, you won't be able to see the head of the harbor. This spot is the gateway to the long, thin barrier beach — the whale's tail — which stretches out to the tip at Great Point and curls around to Coatue, the scalloped barrier beach that forms Nantucket Harbor.

Just beyond the tiny summer colony which is nestled in a grove of Japanese black pines, and the lovely Victorian Wauwinet House, is the Haulover. Years ago, fishermen used to haul their dories over the sandbar (hence, Haulover) to get into Nantucket Harbor without making the long trip around Great Point. Periodically the ocean breaks through, and then the beach builds up again, closing the opening. The ocean broke through again in the spring of 1984.

Quidnet
Quidnet Road

Staying on the paved road, retrace your steps to the intersection of Polpis Road and bear left onto Quidnet Road which dead ends down at the beach. There are cottages here alongside the beach and Sesachacha Pond, but during the whaling and codfishing era, when small boats went out from shore here, this was an active fishing village. A section of the barrier beach separating the pond from the ocean, near the parking lot, belongs to the Nantucket Conservation Foundation. The area is wild and undeveloped and the huge, pink, four-petal Rose Mallows growing around the pond are a lovely sight in midsummer.

Siasconset

Leaving Quidnet, head back toward Polpis on the paved road and go left on the next paved road you come to. This is the Polpis Road which leads to 'Sconset. At the Sankaty Head Golf Club, which is private, you will see the Sankaty Head Lighthouse on your left. It was these sandy cliffs that George Waymouth in 1604 mentioned while he was sailing offshore. The Sankaty Head light is visible 29 miles out at sea.

Siasconset, always pronounced 'Sconset, was settled in the seventeenth century, and some of its tiny houses are the oldest on the Island. It's a village in miniature where doll-sized, grey-weathered cottages with sloping roofs are covered with rambler roses and hollyhocks filling their doorways. Nestled close together on this bluff of land overlooking the sea, the houses are separated by narrow, winding grass paths that enhance the Lilliputian character and charm of the community.

The cottages were first built as one-room fishing shacks by fishermen from town who came to 'Sconset to go offshore for shore whaling and codfishing. They spent the season here, but eventually the wives decided they wanted to join their husbands, so "warts" or small bedrooms were tacked onto the dwellings. They began enclosing the kitchen porches which had wooden chimneys, and as time went on, other additions were added here and there, very casually. Below the town today there is still an area known as Codfish Park.

In the 1880's, Nantucket was having a welcome tourist boom and wealthy residents from town started building summer homes on the edge of the 'Sconset settlement. In 1884 arrangements were made by the owners of the Nantucket Railroad to extend their track out to 'Sconset from Surfside. Their train, *Dionis*, was the pride of Nantucket, and some years later was succeeded by another train called *'Sconset*. Heavy storms kept ruining the track which ran alongshore, so the route was changed to run directly from town out to 'Sconset. Then a new gasoline motor car called *The Bug And The Bird Cage* was put on the run. It flew over the tracks to 'Sconset in 19 minutes and, unfortunately, became so frisky it plummeted off the road one day and was squashed. A successor managed to "turn turtle" on South Beach, but was retrieved and continued in service for several years. Finally a new train, consisting of locomotive, passenger and baggage car, operated until 1917 when the railroad was abandoned.

Before the turn of the century, 'Sconset became a very popular summer colony for theatre personalities from New York City, such as Lillian Russell and Joseph Jefferson. Fortunately they contributed to the preservation of the tiny houses, undoubtedly because of their limited financial means and because of their appreciation of the character of the village. They didn't mind standing in line at the old wooden pump to get their water; the pump, too, has been carefully preserved in the center of 'Sconset.

Marconi established a wireless station in 'Sconset which was the first to participate in reporting maritime news or transmitting calls for help in sea disasters. One of the young operators who worked here was David Sarnoff who later went on to found RCA.

Codfish Park, below the bluff, is just north of the town's public beach where there is a lifeguard on duty. In the center of the village by the rotary there's a catering shop which puts up box lunches to take to the beach, a liquor store, a post office, and a newspaper store. The 'Sconset Casino nearby is a private tennis club which also shows movies that are open to the public.

Siasconset, c.1880

In the 1880's large summer homes were built along the bluff at 'Sconset, and the train ran along the beach in front.

The old wooden well in the center of 'Sconset where residents lined up with buckets was completed in 1776.

Tom Nevers Head
Ocean Avenue

Bear right at the little rotary in the center of the
village of 'Sconset, to take the road along the Atlantic Ocean. Go past the guidepost directing you to
Spain, the next landfall to the East, and on to the
large Coast Guard Station. Just as the road starts to
curve around here, you are facing the south shore.
('Sconset faces East and, when the weather is bad,
gets those Northeasters head on.) The erosion here
is so severe that up to nine acres a year is lost.

Cranberry Bog
Milestone Road

Doubling back, take the Milestone Road, the main
road running from 'Sconset into town. A short distance along this road, on your right, is the dirt road
leading into the cranberry bog which has been in
existence since the seventeenth century. While
cranberries had been used for years as a staple on
sailing ships, it wasn't until the 1850's, after the
whaling and sheep economies had declined, that
they became a cash crop. The Nantucket Cranberry
Company at one time had all four hundred acres
under cultivation, but by the 1960's, low prices
forced the owner to sell. Walter Beinecke, the late
Roy Larsen, a summer resident and former president of Time, Inc., and Arthur Dean, a New York
lawyer, bought the bog and gave it to the Nantucket
Conservation Foundation. Today about one hundred acres are under cultivation, with plans for
more, and the fruit is shipped to the Ocean Spray
Company on Cape Cod. Beehives are placed near
the bog to help with pollination; their honey is sold
on the Island. Profits from the cranberries and
honey go to the Nantucket Conservation Foundation to help with their extraordinarily successful efforts to preserve the land. The bog is not open to
the public.

The ocean can be very rough after an autumn storm.

Surfside
Surfside Road

Continue on Milestone Road toward town, turn left onto Old South Road and immediately right onto Fairgrounds Road. At the next intersection bear left onto Surfside Road that leads on down to the beach. The beach is one of the most popular swimming spots on the Island.

Cisco
Hummock Pond Road

Return toward town on Surfside Road. Opposite the school on your right is Vesper Lane on your left. Take this road and go left again on Hummock Pond Road leading right on down to the popular beach at Cisco. The vast plains to your right, which Thoreau called "a prairie," were used for sheep grazing and were the place where the annual sheepshearing took place. The Miacomet Raceway here has harness races every Wednesday night — an amateur event — and there are public golf courses and tennis courts here. A sign shows the way to Bartlett's famous produce farm that has been in business for years. The fall is so mild on Nantucket, crops that can not grow on Martha's Vineyard or Cape Cod are available. The produce cart which arrives every morning on the cobblestone square in the center of town, and has been an Island institution for years, has an extraordinary selection in the late fall.

Madaket
Madaket Road

Return again towards town and take the first paved road to the left which leads over to the Madaket Road. A left turn leads the traveler down to this charming harbor on the western tip of the island. At the end of the road is a fine public fishing area that is popular for catching bluefish. Across the opening here is Esther Island, the original Old Smith Point before it was cut off by Hurricane Esther in 1971 and renamed. Return from the point on the road that runs alongside Hither Creek. The creek pro-

155

Eel Point

Eel Point, on the northern side of Madaket Harbor, is owned by the Nantucket Conservation Foundation.

vides a fine, protected anchorage for small boats, and at its head is a boatyard. Grey seals from offshore swim up this creek to feed on the herring. Little Neck, on the north side of the creek on Madaket's crescent-shaped harbor, is owned by the Conservation Foundation. Eel Point, on the northern side of Madaket Harbor, is another property of the Conservation Foundation. The currents swirling around the point make swimming very dangerous. There has been an enormous building boom here and houses and cottages are available to rent.

Dionis Beach
Eel Point Road

Return toward town on the Madaket Road, and turn left on the first paved road, clearly marked with a sign, to Dionis Beach. Capaum Pond, the site of the Island's first settlement, is on your right. The paved road ends at the beach which has lovely rolling dunes and gentle surf because it faces Nantucket Sound.

Jetties Beach
North Beach Street

Leaving Dionis and heading back to Madaket Road, take the paved Cliff Road at the intersection to your left and continue back to town. This particular drive through open rolling land offers beautiful vistas of the western end of the Island. You'll come to Maxcy's Pond on your right, and the dirt road just beyond leads over to the Founding Father's Burying Ground. Some of Nantucket's most elegant summer houses are on the bluff overlooking Nantucket Sound in this area. Cliff Road leads to Easton Street, bear left and take your second left on North Beach Street. You double back here, heading out of town until you come to Jetties Beach. This is a large area, with delightful swimming, and because it offers so many conveniences, is extremely popular.

Brant Point

Leaving Jetties Beach, go left on Hulbert Avenue, and follow it to the Brant Point Light and adjacent Coast Guard Station on your left. There have been several lighthouses on this site since the first one built in 1746. That early lighthouse was a lantern hung between two poles. Later lighthouses consisted of larger lanterns on top of a platform, until a regular lighthouse was finally built.

The beach area is small and lacking facilities because the currents can be quite strong. It is really best enjoyed as a spot from which to watch the boats going in and out of Nantucket Harbor.

Follow Easton Street back to town, past Children's Beach to the wharves.

157

Special Events

12

April

Easter Egg Hunt

The Chamber of Commerce sponsors this event on Easter Sunday afternoon. It is open to the public.

Daffodil Festival Weekend

It was in 1974 that Jean MacAusland, the wife of the publisher of *Gourmet Magazine,* originated a Daffodil Exhibit with the Nantucket Garden Club. It gradually became a weekend festival. Now Nantucket annually celebrates the rites of spring the last weekend of April, and it is a great tribute to Jean

MacAusland. Over a million daffodils line the road-sides and the town itself bursts into bloom. Prizes are awarded for the most attractive shop window. There's an Antique Car Parade, with autos decorated with daffodils, from town out to Siasconset for a Tailgate Picnic on Saturday (with Sunday the raindate). On Saturday night, there's a Daffodil Ball at the Harbor House. On Monday and Tuesday there is an exhibition and judging of flowers and arrangements at the Harbor House by the National Daffodil Society.

Library Open House

The Maria Mitchell Association Library, in observance of National Library Week, holds an annual Open House to mark the end of winter. Exhibits show the early arrival of Island birds, flowers, and plants, as well as what constellations to look for in the spring sky.

May

Artists' Association Craft Show

This craft show at the Kenneth Taylor Gallery on Straight Wharf goes on for the entire month of May. The work of Island artists, potters, sculptors, and other craftsmen is on exhibit.

Ten-Mile Bike Race

In mid-May the Chamber of Commerce sponsors its annual ten-mile bike race around the Island.

Memorial Day Weekend

To many summer and year-round residents, this weekend is when the season begins. Homeowners return to open their houses for the summer, ferry reservations for a car are impossible unless they were made months in advance, and the hotels are filled. The Easy Striders Annual Sealegs Road Race, which is five miles long, takes place on Sunday of this weekend. At the Kenneth Taylor Gallery, the

Artists' Association sponsors a Junior Artists' Show displaying the work of the local schoolchildren.

June

Cranberry Classic Road Race

This annual event in mid-June is a road race for 300 joggers. It begins at the Wauwinet House at the head of Nantucket Harbor and finishes in town.

July

Fourth of July

There's a very colorful and well-attended Independence Day Parade followed by the fireworks display in the evening at Jetties Beach. Check the calendar of events for the time and route of this delightful small-town parade.

Flower Show

The Nantucket Garden Club has its annual Green Thumb and Flower Show at the Kenneth Taylor Gallery on Straight Wharf early in July. The Garden Club doesn't have its own building, and its meetings are held in the Nantucket Elementary School.

Antiques Show

The annual Nantucket Antiques Show which is held at the elementary school on Atlantic Avenue, the road to Surfside, gives some of its proceeds to the Nantucket schools. Because there are so many fine antique shops on the Island, the selection at the show is excellent, and off-Island dealers also participate. It is held in the middle of the month.

Annual House Tour

The Nantucket Garden Club sponsors the annual house tour which takes place each year at the end of July. The houses open for the tour are private homes, not those belonging to the Historical Asso-

STEVEN HEASLIP

**Congregational
Meeting House**
*Rose Sunday takes place
in the Congregational
Meeting House in July
every year.*

ciation. Most of them are old, although some might be modern, and they are different each year. They are geographically grouped together so one may take a cab or bus to a certain area, buy a ticket at the door of one of the houses, and easily walk to the others. The proceeds from this tour go to the Garden Club.

Rose Sunday

In the very beautiful Congregational Church on Centre Street, the charming custom of Rose Sunday takes place. The inspiration of a former pastor, the church is filled with roses which thrive in Nantucket's warm climate and misty air.

August

Sidewalk Art Show

For over fifty years the Artists' Association has had an annual art show at the foot of Main Street's cobblestone square on Broad Street in front of the Town and County Building. The works of many Island artists are on display in this show.

Billfish Tournament

The Nantucket Angler's Club, a private fishing club, sponsors a tournament each July which is open to the public. Limited to fifty boats, the sports fishermen go offshore for swordfish and marlin, and prizes are awarded.

Beaux Arts Ball

The Artists' Association holds this ball annually at the Harbor House to raise money for its organization. It is open to the public.

Theatre Workshop Antiques Show

The Theatre Workshop puts on an antiques show each summer to raise money for its productions. It is held at the elementary school.

Sandcastle Contest

The Chamber of Commerce sponsors this event each summer at Jetties Beach. It's extremely popular with children, but many adults also participate, creating large fanciful sculptures which last until the incoming tide takes them away.

Tree Fund Cocktail Party

Not many places in the country have benefit cocktail parties for trees, but they have always been a precious commodity on this windswept island. Herman Melville, author of *Moby Dick,* called it an "elbow of sand" where ". . . pieces of wood in Nantucket are carried about like bits of the true cross in Rome; that people there plant toadstools before their houses, to get under the shade in summertime . . ." Held at the White Elephant, this cocktail party and fashion show is for a very worthy cause, and the proceeds are used to buy seedlings and larger trees.

Carnival

Nantucket doesn't have a country fair anymore, but once a summer a visiting carnival arrives. It used to be behind the First National Store on Sparks Avenue. In 1983 it was held at Tom Nevers.

September

Seafest

Fried clams, oysters, broiled monkfish, tilefish, and squid are just some of the seafood items to try at this annual festival held on Children's Beach where upwards of 5,000 persons gather. The purpose of the event is to try to interest the public in eating new and unfamiliar types of fish as the old ones, such as swordfish and bass, become increasingly scarce. There are also marine biology displays at this festival. It's an interesting fish fair in a delightful setting alongshore, and a beautiful season of the year on the Island.

October

Columbus Day Road Race

Columbus Day is another very big weekend on Nantucket, the end of the season for many people. Sponsored by the Chamber of Commerce, this ten-mile road race starts at Siasconset Village, is run over the Polpis Road, and finishes at the Nantucket Boys Club on Sparks Avenue. There are five divisions of joggers.

Art Auction

The Artists' Association winds up the season with an auction at the Kenneth Taylor Gallery to raise money for its organization.

LARRY CRONIN

Christmas Shoppers Stroll

The Shoppers Stroll is a very popular event held every year on the second Saturday in December.

Halloween Costume Party

The Harbor House puts on a Halloween Costume
Party that is attended by many Islanders. Prizes are
awarded in various categories.

November

There are no special events in the month of November, other than the usual scheduled programs
(listed under Leisure Activities). However, it should
be noted that Nantucket is lovely this time of year; a
reservation at the Coffin House for Thanksgiving
Dinner should be made months in advance, and the
hotels are crowded with many people attracted to a
country holiday in this Island setting. The restaurants not only feature traditional food, but also native pheasant and quail.

December

Christmas Shoppers Stroll

It has been a decade since the first Christmas Shoppers Stroll, held on the second Saturday in December, and the influx of people to this holiday setting,
which looks like a Charles Dickens Christmas card,
increases every year. Everyone seems to want to
join in to make it a very festive event. The town
highway department raises the bricks along Main
Street from the Pacific Bank down to the harborfront and plants live Christmas trees the whole
length of both sides of the street. They are all
lighted and decorated by the schoolchildren who
use everything from cranberries to painted scallop
shells as ornaments. Carolers' voices ring out the
glad tidings from the steps of the bank at the top of
the square, roasting chestnuts are offered by the
Boy Scouts, there are wandering minstrels and hot
mulled cider, and Santa and Mrs. Claus arrive by
horse-drawn sled. Every window in all the buildings is lighted with candles, and the old gas street-
lamps lining the cobblestone square are decked out

in pine and red ribbons. Late in the day all the tree lights are turned on, and the visitor is set back a century as he looks up the street at this charming nineteenth-century Christmas scene. Only the electricity is a twentieth-century intrusion. The pealing of church bells completes this delightful Christmas event.

Community Christmas Celebration

The Christmas Pageant at the strikingly beautiful Old North Church on Christmas Eve is a very moving play of the Christmas story put on by the Theatre Workshop, with accompaniment by the Community Chorus.

Epilogue

Nantucket is fragile, very fragile. The water table, the harbor, the marine life, and tourist activity — the delicate balance between nature and people must be cautiously weighed. The Island is so appealing and popular, the number of visitors increases each season, and measures to protect the Island's character have to be taken. That is why the Chamber of Commerce and others urge you not to bring your car if you're staying in the center of town. In January, 1984, The Nantucket Land Bank, a plan designed to impose a two-percent tax on all land transactions was passed overwhelmingly. The proceeds from this tax will be used to buy Island property for public use, while the enormous effort on the part of both native Islanders and summer residents to keep things in balance and land left open, continues.

It is difficult to even imagine what Nantucket would be like without the enormous contributions in time, money, land, and buildings by so many native Islanders and summer residents. Because of their diligence and dedication, one third of the Island is now preserved and protected from development, and twelve buildings and the Nantucket Lightship have been preserved for the public. It is a singular achievement, and the vast tracts of open land and beach are open for nature walks or fishing. The Nantucket Historical Association owns and maintains the buildings, and the Nantucket Conservation Foundation supervises the maintenance of over forty properties. These acquisitions of land and buildings have protected Nantucket from losing its character and being overrun with housing developments, her marshes and moors destroyed. Both organizations welcome any contributions to help maintain this delicate balance between nature and man.

It is very important for you, the visitor, to show as much consideration for the Island, which belongs to someone else, as if it were your own. You should realize you are an off-Islander from the "mainland" or "continent." Like all persons living on islands, Nantucketers have a special pride and sense of place, an Island consciousness with deep roots which is, of course, one of the reasons for the Island's great attraction. Consideration of the Nantucketer's attitude, as you share the attributes of his home, is recommended of all visitors. There are many ways you can be helpful while you are enjoying your vacation: Leave your car on the mainland if possible; don't pick or dig up ANY wildflowers; leave all small shellfish entirely alone and encourage your children to do the same; do not trample the dunes and plant life growing on them; and pick up your own litter.

The problem of preserving a bit of America's heritage was perhaps best expressed a century ago when a beautiful sailing ship was leaving South Street Seaport in New York on her maiden voyage. The builder turned to the ship's master and said, "Take good care of her, Mister. When she's gone, there'll be no more like her."

When you visit Nantucket, take good care of her, for when she's gone, there'll be no more like her.

When you leave Nantucket, be sure to make a wish as you cruise past Brant Point Light.

171

INDEX

Numbers in italics refer to pictures

184